Berlitz®

Swedish

phrase book & dictionary

Berlitz Publishing
New York   London   Singapore

Contacting the Editors
Every effort has been made to provide accurate information in this publication, but changes are inevitable. The publisher cannot be responsible for any resulting loss, inconvenience or injury. We would appreciate it if readers would call our attention to any errors or outdated information. We also welcome your suggestions; if you come across a relevant expression not in our phrase book, please contact us at: **comments@berlitzpublishing.com**

All Rights Reserved
© 2007 Berlitz Publishing/APA Publications (UK) Ltd.
Berlitz Trademark Reg. U.S. Patent Office and other countries. Marca Registrada. Used under license from Berlitz Investment Corporation.

Eleventh Printing: March 2012
Printed in China

Publishing Director: Mina Patria
Commissioning Editor: Kate Drynan
Editorial Assistant: Sophie Cooper
Translation: updated by Wordbank
Cover Design: Beverley Speight
Interior Design: Beverley Speight
Production Manager: Raj Trivedi
Picture Researcher: Lucy Johnston
Cover Photo: Julian Love/APA except 'currency' image iStockphoto

Interior Photos: Kevin Cummins/APA 39, 51; Ming Tang Evans/APA 76, 100; David Hall/APA 96; iStockphoto 16, 146, 156, 161, 162,165, 173, 174; Lucy Johnston/APA 187; Julian Love/APA 1, 14, 18, 27, 57, 61, 87, 99, 109, 110, 112, 114, 117, 120, 122, 124, 128, 131, 140, 154, 170, 179; Frank Noon/APA 95; Jonas Overodder/Imagebank.Sweden.SE 90; Sylvaine Poitau/APA 103; Beverley Speight 52; Corrie Wingate/APA 89; Gregory Wrona/APA 93, 107

Contents

Pronunciation	7	Vowels	9
Consonants	8	How to use this Book	12

Survival

Arrival & Departure	**15**	Parking	36
ESSENTIAL	15	Breakdown & Repair	37
Border Control	15	Accidents	37
Money	**17**	**Places to Stay**	**38**
ESSENTIAL	17	ESSENTIAL	38
At the Bank	17	Somewhere to Stay	39
		At the Hotel	39
Getting Around	**20**	Price	40
ESSENTIAL	20	Preferences	42
Tickets	21	Questions	42
Plane	22	Problems	43
Airport Transfer	22	Checking Out	44
Checking In	23	Renting	45
Luggage	25	Domestic Items	46
Finding your Way	25	At the Hostel	47
Train	26	Going Camping	48
Departures	26		
On Board	28	**Communications**	**49**
Bus	28	ESSENTIAL	49
Subway	29	Online	50
Boat & Ferry	31	Social Media	51
Taxi	31	Phone	53
Bicycle & Motorbike	33	Telephone Etiquette	54
Car Hire	33	Fax	55
Fuel Station	34	Post	56
Asking Directions	35		

Food & Drink

Eating Out   **58**
ESSENTIAL   58
Where to Eat   59
Reservations & Preferences   60
How to Order   61
Cooking Methods   62
Dietary Requirements   63
Dining with Children   64
How to Complain   64
Paying   64

Meals & Cooking   **65**
Breakfast   65
Appetizers   67
Soup   68
Fish & Seafood   68
Meat & Poultry   71

Vegetables & Staples   74
Fruit   78
Cheese   79
Dessert   80
Sauces & Condiments   81
At the Market   81
In the Kitchen   83

Drinks   **84**
ESSENTIAL   84
Non-alcoholic Drinks   85
Aperitifs, Cocktails & Liqueurs   87
Beer   88
Wine   88

On the Menu   **89**

People

Conversation   **115**
ESSENTIAL   115
Language Difficulties   116
Making Friends   117
Travel Talk   118
Personal   118
Work & School   119
Weather   120

Romance   **121**
ESSENTIAL   121
The Dating Game   121
Accepting & Rejecting   122
Getting Intimate   123
Sexual Preferences   123

Leisure Time

Sightseeing **125**
ESSENTIAL 125
Tourist Information 125
On Tour 125
Seeing the Sights 127
Religious Sites 128

Shopping **129**
ESSENTIAL 129
At the Shops 129
Ask an Assistant 131
Personal Preferences 132
Paying & Bargaining 133
Making a Complaint 134
Services 134
Hair & Beauty 135
Antiques 136
Clothing 136
Colors 137
Clothes & Accessories 138

Fabric 139
Shoes 140
Sizes 140
Newsagent & Tobacconist 141
Photography 141
Souvenirs 142

Sport & Leisure **144**
ESSENTIAL 144
Watching Sport 145
Playing Sport 146
At the Beach/Pool 147
Winter Sports 148
Out in the Country 149

Going Out **151**
ESSENTIAL 151
Entertainment 151
Nightlife 152

5

Special Requirements

Business Travel **155**
ESSENTIAL 155
On Business 155

Traveling with Children **157**
ESSENTIAL 157
Out & About 158

Baby Essentials 159
Babysitting 159
Health & Emergency 160

Disabled Travelers **160**
ESSENTIAL 160
Asking for Assistance 161

In an Emergency

Emergencies	**163**	Basic Supplies	173
ESSENTIAL	163		
		The Basics	**175**
Police	**164**	Grammar	175
ESSENTIAL	164	Numbers	179
Crime & Lost Property	164	ESSENTIAL	179
		Ordinal Numbers	180
Health	**166**	Time	181
ESSENTIAL	166	ESSENTIAL	181
Finding a Doctor	166	Days	182
Symptoms	167	ESSENTIAL	182
Conditions	167	Dates	182
Treatment	168	Months	182
Hospital	169	Seasons	183
Dentist	169	Holidays	183
Gynecologist	169	Conversion Tables	185
Optician	170	Kilometers to Miles Conversions	185
Payment & Insurance	170	Measurement	185
Pharmacy	171	Temperature	186
ESSENTIAL	171	Oven Temperature	186
What to Take	172		

Dictionary

English–Swedish Dictionary	188	Swedish–English Dictionary	206

Pronunciation

This section is designed to familiarize you with the sounds of Swedish using our simplified phonetic transcription. You'll find the pronunciation of the Swedish letters and sounds explained below, together with their 'imitated' equivalents. To use this system, found throughout the phrase book, simply read the pronunciation as if it were English, noting any special rules below.

The Swedish alphabet has 29 letters, the last three of which are the vowels **å**, **ä** and **ö**. Unlike English, the letter **y** is a vowel, meaning that Swedish has nine vowels. Swedish vowels are pure vowel sounds, as opposed to being a combination of two sounds (diphthongs) as they often are in English. Diphthongs occur only in dialects such as **Gotländska** (spoken on the island of Gotland), **Skånska** (spoken in the southern province of Skåne) and **Dalmål** (spoken in Dalarna, a province roughly in the middle of the country.)

Swedish has very consistent rules with respect to the sounding of individual letters, i.e. all the letters should be pronounced distinctly, even vowels and consonants at the ends of words. The Swedish language is often referred to as a 'musical' language due to the fact that the intonation and rhythm moves up and down, giving the language a musical quality. Despite this stress, pronunciation is quite consistent. Most words with two or more syllables have primary stress on the first syllable of the word, and this can be followed by a secondary stress on the second syllable. There are also a number of words with two or more syllables which do not have stress on the first syllable, but often on the last. Stress has been noted in the phonetic transcription with underlining.

Consonants

Letter	Approximate Pronunciation	Symbol	Example	Pronunciation
c	like s in sit	**s**	**cykel**	_sew_·kerl*
g	1. before o, å, a and u, like g in get	**g**	**gata**	_gah_·ta
	2. before i, e, ö and ä, like y in yet	**y**	**get**	yet
	3. after r and l, like y in yet	**y**	**borg**	bohry
j	1. soft, like y in yet	**y**	**jag**	yahg
	2. after r and l, like y in yet	**y**	**familj**	fah·_mihly_
k	1. before o, å, a and u, like k in keep	**k**	**katt**	kat
	2. before i, e, ö and ä, like ch in chew		**köpa**	_chur_·pa
q	like k in keep	**k**	**Blomquist**	_bloom_·kvihst
r	strong, almost trilled, r		**röd**	rurd
s	like s in see	**s**	**sitta**	_siht_·a
w	like v in very	**v**	**wennergren**	_vehn_·eh·_grehn_
z	like s in suit	**s**	**zebra**	_see_·bra

Letters b, d, f, h, m, n, p, t, v and x are pronounced as in English.

*Bold indicates a lengthening of the sound — emphasis on the vowel sound.

Consonant Clusters

Letter	Approximate Pronunciation	Symbol	Example	Pronunciation
ch	like sh in ship	**sh**	**check**	*shehk*
ck	like ck in tick	**k**	**flicka**	*flih•ka*
dj, gj, hj, lj	like y in yet	**y**	**djur**	*yeur*
sj, skj, stj, sch, ch	like sh in shop	**sh**	**sjal**	*shahl*
sk	1. before o, å, a and u, like sk in skip	**sk**	**skala**	*skah•la*
	2. before i, e, ö and ä, like sh in ship	**sh**	**skära**	*shai•ra*
tj	like sh followed by ch	**shch**	**tjock**	*shchohk*

Vowels

Letter	Approximate Pronunciation	Symbol	Example	Pronunciation
a	1. when long, like a in father	**ah**	**dag**	*dahg*
	2. when short, like a in cat	**a**	**katt**	*kat*
e	1. when long, like ee in beer	**ee**	**veta**	*vee•ta*
	2. when short, like e in fell	**eh**	**ett**	*eht*
	Approximate			

Letter	Approximate Pronunciation	Symbol	Example	Pronunciation
i	1. when long, like ee in see	ee	bil	beel
	2. when short, like i in bit	ih	mitt	miht
o	1. when long, like oa in coat	oa	sko	skoa
	2. like the exclamation oh	oh	font	fohnt
u	1. when long, eu in feud	eu	ruta	reu·ta
	2. when short, like u in up	uh	uppe	uh·per
y	like ew in new	ew	byta	bew·ta
å	1. when long, like oa in oar	oa	gå	goa
	2. when short, like o in hot	oh	åtta	oh·ta
ä	1. when long, like ai in air	ai	här	hair
	2. when short, like e in set	eh	säng	sehng
ö	1. when long, like u in cure	ur	smör	smur
	2. when short, like u in nut	uh	rött	ruhrt

Swedish vowels are divided into two groups: hard and soft. **A, o, u** and **å** are hard vowels; **e, i, y, ä** and **ö** are soft vowels. Vowels can also be pronounced either long or short. When a vowel is pronounced 'long' the sound is longer, but also more open and rounder. The 'short' vowel sounds are more closed, literally a 'shorter' sound than a long vowel. An easy rule to remember is that if the vowel is followed by a single consonant, as in **stad** (city), it is long. If the vowel is followed by a double consonant, as in **katt** (cat), the vowel is short. The exception to this rule is with the consonants **m** and **n**.

Swedish is spoken throughout Sweden as well as in the coastal regions of Finland and Estonia. While written Swedish has been standardized, there are characteristic spoken dialects in certain regions such as Gotland, Skåne and Dalarna. Other languages, in addition to Swedish, are also spoken in Sweden, such as Finnish, which is spoken in some communities in Northern Sweden, and the Sámi (Lappish) languages, which are spoken in Sámi communities throughout Northern Norway, Sweden, Finland and Russia. Swedish, Norwegian, Danish, Icelandic and Faroese (spoken on the Faroe Islands) are all derived from Old Norse, the language spoken prior to the Viking Age. Over time, the Scandinavian languages developed from this common language. Danish, Norwegian and Swedish are separate and distinct languages but remain close enough that they are mutually intelligible. The Finnish and Sámi languages belong to a different language family, to which Hungarian also belongs.

How to use this Book

Sometimes you see two alternatives separated by a slash. Choose the one that's right for your situation.

ESSENTIAL

I'm here on vacation [holiday]/business	**Jag är här på semester/affärsresa.** *yahg air hair poa seh-mehs-ter/a-fairs-ree-sa*
I'm going to...	**Jag ska resa till...** *yahg skah ree-sa tihl...*
I'm staying at hotel/youth hostel.	**Jag bor på hotell/vandrarhem.** *yahg boar pao hoh-tehl/vahnd-rar-hehm*

Words you may see are shown in YOU MAY SEE boxes.

YOU MAY SEE...

TULL	customs
TAXFRIA VAROR	duty-free goods
VAROR ATT FÖRTULLA	goods to declare

Any of the words or phrases listed can be plugged into the sentence below.

Watching Sport

When's...?	**När börjar...?** *nair bur-yar...*
the basketball game	**basketboll matchen** *bahs-keht-bohl-ma-shchehn*
the cycling race	**cykeltävlingen** *sew-kehl-taiv-lihng-ehn*
the golf tournament	**golfspelet** *golf-spee-leht*
the soccer [football] game	**fotbollsmatchen** *foat-bohls-ma-shchehn*

Swedish phrases appear in purple.

Read the simplified pronunciation as if it were English. For more on pronunciation, see page 7.

Personal

I'm...	**Jag är...** *yahg air...*
single	**ogift** *oa·yift*
in a relationship	**i ett förhållande** *ee eht furr·hoal·an·der*
married	**gift** *yihft*
divorced	**skild** *shihld*
separated	**separerad** *seh·pa·ree·rad*
I'm a widow/widower.	**Jag är änka/änkling.** *yahg air ehng·ka/ehngk·lihng*

For Numbers, see page 179.

Related phrases can be found by going to the page number indicated.

Swedes shake hands when greeting someone and when saying goodbye; this holds for meeting new people but is also often the case with colleagues or acquaintances.

Information boxes contain relevant country, culture and language tips.

Expressions you may hear are shown in You May Hear boxes.

YOU MAY HEAR...

Jag talar bara lite engelska. *yahg tah·lar bah·ra lee·ter ehng·ehl·ska*
I speak only a little English.

Jag talar inte engelska. *yahg tah·lar in·ter ehng·ehl·ska*
I don't speak English.

Color-coded side bars identify each section of the book.

Survival

Arrival & Departure   15
Money   17
Getting Around   20
Places to Stay   38
Communications   49

Arrival & Departure

ESSENTIAL

I'm here on vacation [holiday]/business.	**Jag är här på semester/affärsresa.** *Yahg air hair poa seh·mehs·ter/a·fairs·ree·sa*
I'm going to...	**Jag ska resa till...** *yahg skah ree·sa tihl...*
I'm staying at a hotel/youth hostel.	**Jag bor på hotell/vandrarhem.** *yahg boar poa hoh·tehl/vahnd·rar·hehm*

YOU MAY HEAR...

Er biljett/Ert pass, tack. *eer bihl·yeht/ eert pas tak*
Your ticket/passport, please.

Vad är syftet med ert besök? *vahd air sewf·tet meed ehrt beh·surk*
What's the purpose of your visit?

Var bor du? *vahr boar deu*
Where are you staying?

Hur länge ska du stanna? *heur lehng·er skah deu stan·a*
How long are you staying?

Vem är du här med? *vehm air deu hair meed*
Who are you here with?

Border Control

I'm just passing through.	**Jag är bara på genomresa.** *yahg air bah·ra poa ye·nohm·ree·sa*
I would like to declare...	**Jag skulle vilja förtulla...** *yahg skuh·ler vihl·ya furr·tuh·la...*
I have nothing to declare.	**Jag har inget att förtulla.** *yahg hahr ihng·eht at furr·tuh·la*

YOU MAY HEAR...

Har du något att förtulla?
hahr deu noa·goht at furr·tuh·la
Du måste betala tull för det här.
deu mos·ter beh·tah·la tuhl furr dee hair
Var snäll och öppna den här väskan.
vahr snehl ohk urp·na dehn hair vehs·kan

Anything to
declare?
You must pay duty
on this.
Please open this bag.

YOU MAY SEE...

TULL	customs
TAXFRIA VAROR	duty-free goods
VAROR ATT FÖRTULLA	goods to declare
INGET ATT FÖRTULLA	nothing to declare
PASSKONTROLL	passport control
POLIS	police

Money

ESSENTIAL

Where's…?	**Var ligger…?** *vahr lih·gehr…*
the ATM	**bankomaten** *bank·oa·mah·tehn*
the bank	**banken** _bank·ehn_
the currency exchange office	**växelkontoret** _vehx·ehl·kohn·toar·eht_
What time does the bank open/close?	**När öppnar/stänger banken?** *nair urp·nahr/ stehng·ehr bank·ehn*
I'd like to change dollars/pounds into kronor.	**Jag skulle vilja växla dollar/pund till kronor.** *yahg skuh·ler vihl·ya vehx·la doh·lar/ pund tihl kroa·nohr*
I want to cash some traveler's checks [cheques].	**Jag skulle vilja lösa in några resecheckar.** *yahg skuh·ler vihl·yalur·sa ihn noa·gra ree·seh·sheh·kar*

At the Bank

Can I exchange foreign currency here?	**Kan jag växla pengar här?** *kan yahg vehx·la pehng·ar hair*
What's the exchange rate?	**Vad är växelkursen?** *vahd air vehx·ehl·keur·shehn*
I think there's a mistake.	**Jag tror det är ett misstag.** *Yahg troar dee air eht mis·tagh*
How much is the fee?	**Hur mycket är expeditionsavgiften?** *Heur mew·ker air ehx·peh·dee·shoans·afv·yihf·tehn*
I've lost my traveler's checks.	**Jag har tappat mina resecheckar.** *Yahg hahr ta·pat mee·na ree·seh·sheh·kar*

YOU MAY SEE...

SÄTT IN KORTET	insert card
AVBESTÄLLA	cancel
RENSA	clear
ENTER	enter
PINKOD	PIN
TA UT	withdraw
FRÅN CHEKKONTO	from checking [current] account
FRÅN SPARKONTO	from savings account
KVITTOT	receipt

I've lost my card.	**Jag har tappat mitt kort.**	*yahg hahr ta·pat miht koart*
My credit cards have been stolen.	**Mina kreditkort är stulna.**	*mee·na kreh·deet·koart air steul·na*
My card doesn't work.	**Mitt kort fungerar inte.**	*miht koart fuhn·gee·rar ihn·te*
The ATM ate my card.	**Uttagsautomaten tog mitt kort.**	*eut·tahgs·ah·toa·mah·tehn toagh mith koart.*

For Numbers, see page 179.

YOU MAY SEE...

Unlike the majority of other European Union countries, Sweden has not adopted the euro as its national currency. Sweden's monetary unit is the **krona** (singular) or **kronor** (plural) abbreviated to **SEK**.
The **krona** is divided into **öre**.
Coins: 50 **öre**, 1 **krona**, 5 and 10 **kronor**
Banknotes: 20, 50, 100, 500 and 1000 **kronor**

Cash can be obtained from a **Bankomat** (ATM) with MasterCard, Visa, Eurocard, American Express and other international credit cards or with a debit card. It is also possible to exchange traveler's checks in Sweden. In recent years, it has become quite common for the banks to refer customers with traveler's checks to the nearest **växelkontor** (currency exchange business) such as Forex or X-Change. These businesses are often located near or in points of departure/arrival such as airports or train stations, but can also be found in city centers. Remember to bring your passport with you for identification when you want to exchange money or cash traveler's checks. Most banks close at 3:00 p.m., though some are open later one day a week, often on Thursdays.

Getting Around

ESSENTIAL

How do I get to town?	**Hur kommer jag till staden?** heur <u>koh</u>•mehr yahg tihl <u>stahd</u>•ehn
Where is…?	**Var ligger…?** vahr <u>lih</u>•gehr…
the airport	**flygplatsen** <u>flewg</u>•plats•ehn
the train [railway] station	**järnvägsstationen** yairn•vehgs•sta•<u>shoa</u>•nehn
the bus station	**bussterminalen** bus•tehr•<u>mee</u>•nah•lehn
the subway [underground] station	**tunnelbanestationen** teu•nehl•bah•neh•sta•<u>shoan</u>•ehn
How far is it?	**Hur långt är det?** heur loangt air dee
Where can I buy tickets?	**Var kan jag köpa biljetter?** vahr kan yahg <u>chur</u>•pa bil•<u>yeht</u>•tehr
A one-way [single]/ round-trip [return].	**Enkel./Retur.** <u>ehng</u>•kehl/reh•<u>teur</u>
How much does it cost?	**Hur mycket kostar det?** heur <u>mew</u>•ker <u>kos</u>•tar dee
Are there any discounts?	**Finns det några rabatter?** fihns dee <u>noa</u>•gra ra•<u>bat</u>•ehr
Which gate?	**Vid vilken gate?** veed <u>vihl</u>•kehn gayt
Which line?	**Vilken kö?** <u>vihl</u>•kehn kur
Which platform?	**Vilken plattform?** <u>vihl</u>•kehn <u>plat</u>•fohrm
Where can I get a taxi?	**Var kan jag få tag på en taxi?** vahr kan yahg foa tahg poa ehn <u>tax</u>•ee
Please take me to this address.	**Var snäll och kör mig till denna address.** vahr snehl ohk churr may tihl <u>deh</u>•na ad•<u>rehs</u>
Where can I rent a car?	**Var kan jag hyra en bil?** vahr kan yahg <u>hew</u>•ra ehn beel

I'd like a map. **Jag skulle vilja ha en karta.** *Yahg <u>skuh</u>•ler <u>vihl</u>•ya h**ah** ehn <u>kahr</u>•ta*

Tickets

When is...to	**När går...till Uppsala?** *nair goar...tihl <u>uhp</u>•sah•la Uppsala?*
the (first) bus	**(första) bussen** <u>(furs</u>•ta) *buhs•ehn*
the (next) flight	**(nästa) flyg** <u>(nehs</u>•ta) *flewg*
the (last) train	**(sista) tåget** <u>(sihs</u>•ta) <u>toa</u>•geht
Where can I buy tickets?	**Var kan jag köpa biljetter?** *vahr kan yahg <u>chur</u>•pa bihl•<u>yeht</u>•er*
One ticket/Two tickets, please.	**En biljett/Två biljetter, tack.** *ehn bil•<u>yet</u>/tv**oa** bil•<u>yeht</u>•er tak*
For today/tomorrow.	**Till dagens/imorgon.** *tihl <u>dah</u>•gens/ee•<u>mo</u>•ron*
...ticket.	**...biljett.** *...bihl•<u>yeht</u>*
A one-way [single]	**En enkel** *ehn <u>ehng</u>•kehl*
A return-trip	**En retur** *ehn reh•<u>teur</u>*
A first class	**En första klass** *ehn <u>furr</u>•sta klas*
A business class	**En i affärsklass** *Ehn ee a•fairs•klas*
An economy class	**En turist klass** *ehn tuh•<u>rihst</u> klas*
How much does it cost?	**Hur mycket kostar det?** *heur <u>mew</u>•ker <u>kos</u>•tar **dee***
Is there a discount for...?	**Blir det rabatt för...?** *bleer d**ee** ra•<u>bat</u> furr...*
children	**barn** *bahrn*
students	**studerande** <u>steu</u>•d**ee**•ran•der
senior citizens	**pensionärer** *pan•sh**oa**•<u>nair</u>•ehr*
tourists	**turister** *tuh•rihst•ehr*
The express bus/express train, please.	**Expressbussen/expresståget, tack.** *Ehx•prehs•buhs•ehn/ehx•prehs•t**oa**•geht, tak*

The local bus/train, please.	**Lokalbussen/tåget, tack.** *Loh•kahl•buhs•en/ toa•geht, tak*
I have an e-ticket.	**Jag har en e-biljett.** *yahg hahr ehn ee•bihl•yet*
Can I buy a ticket on the bus/train?	**Kan jag köpa en biljett på bussen/tåget?** *kan yahg chur•pa ehn bihl•yeht poa bus•ehn/toa•geht*
Do I have to stamp the ticket before boarding?	**Ska jag stämpla biljetten innan jag går ombord?** *Skah yahg stehm•pla bil•yet•ehn•ihn•ahn•yahg•goar•ohm•bohrd*
How long is this ticket valid?	**Hur länge gäller denna biljett?** *Heur lehng•er yeh•lehr deh•na bihl•yet*
Can I return on the same ticket?	**Kan jag åka tillbaka med samma biljett?** *Kahn yahg oak•ha tihl•bah•ka mehd sam•a bihl•yet*
I'd like to...my reservation.	**Jag skulle vilja...min bokning.** *Yahg skuh•ler vihl•ya...mihn boak•nihng*
cancel	**avbeställa** *afv•beh•steh•la*
change	**ändra** *ehn•dra*
confirm	**bekräfta** *beh•krehf•ta*

Plane

Airport Transfer

How much is a taxi to the airport?	**Vad kostar en taxi till flygplatsen?** *Vahd kos•tar ehn tax•ee tihl flewg•plat•sehn*
To...Airport, please.	**Till...Flygplats, tack.** *tihl...flewg•plats tak*
My airline is...	**Mitt flygbolag är...** *miht flewg•boa•lahg air...*
My flight leaves at...	**Mitt flyg avgår klockan...** *miht flewg afv•goar kloh•kan...*
I'm in a rush.	**Jag har bråttom.** *yahg hahr broa•tohm*
Can you take an alternate route?	**Kan du köra någon annan väg?** *kan deu chur•ra noa•gohn an•nan vehg*
Can you drive faster/slower?	**Kan du köra lite fortare/långsammare?** *kan deu chur•ra lee•ter foar•ta•rer/loang•sam•a•rer*

YOU MAY HEAR...

Vilket flygbolag reser du med? *vihl·keht flewg·boa·lahg ree·sehr deu meed* — What airline are you flying?

Inrikes eller utrikes? *in·ree·kehs ehl·er eut·ree·kehs* — Domestic or International?

Vilken terminal? *vihl·kehn tehr·mee·nahl* — What terminal?

Checking In

Where is check-in?	**Var är incheckningen?** *vahr air in·shehk·nihng·ehn*	
My name is...	**Jag heter...** *yahg hee·ter...*	
I'm going to...	**Jag ska resa till...** *yahg skah ree·sa tihl...*	
I have...	**Jag har....** *Yahg hahr...*	
one suitcase	**en resväska** *ehn rehs·vehs·ka*	
two suitcases	**två resväskor** *tvoh rehs·vehs·kohr*	
one piece of hand luggage	**ett handbagage** *eht hand ·ba·gah·sh*	
How much luggage is allowed?	**Hur mycket gratis bagage får man ha?** *heur mew·ker grah·tihs ba·goash foar man hah*	

YOU MAY SEE...

ANKOMST	arrivals
AVGÅNG	departures
BAGAGEUTLÄMNING	baggage claim
INRIKESFLYG	domestic flights
UTRIKESFLYG	international flights
CHECKA IN	check-in
CHECKA IN E-BILJETT	e-ticket check-in
AVGÅNGSGATER	departure gates

Is that pounds or kilos?	**Är det i pund eller kilo?** *Air deht ee pund ehl·er cheeh·loh*
Which terminal/gate does flight... leave from?	**Vid vilken terminal/gate går flygnummer...?** *veed vihl·kehn tehr·mee·nahl/gayt goar flewg·nuhm·ehr...*
I'd like a window/an aisle seat.	**Jag skulle vilja ha en fönsterplats/plats i mittgången.** *yahg skuh·ler vihl·ya hah ehn furns·tehr·plats/plats ee miht·goang·ehn*

YOU MAY HEAR...

Nästa! *nehs·ta*	Next!
Er biljett/Ert pass, tack. *eer bihl·yet/ eert pas tak*	Your ticket/passport, please.
Hur mycket bagage har du? *heur mew·ker ba·goash hahr deu*	How much luggage do you have?
Du har övervikt. *deu hahr ur·vehr·vikt*	You have excess luggage.
Det där är för tungt/för stort handbagage. *dee dair air furr teungt/furr stoart hand·ba·goash*	That's too heavy/large for a carry-on [to carry on board].
Packade du väskorna själv? *pa·ka·der deu vehs·kohr·na shehlv*	Did you pack these bags yourself?
Har någon gett er något att ta med? *hahr noa·gohn yeht eer noa·goht at tah meed*	Did anyone give you anything to carry?
Töm era fickor, tack. *turm ee·ra fihk·ohr tak*	Empty your pockets, please.
Ta av er skorna, tack. *ta afv eer skoar·na tak*	Take off your shoes, please.
Nu är ni välkommna att borda flight nummer... *neu air nee vail·kohm·na at bohr·da flajt nuhm·ehr...*	Now boarding flight...

When do we leave/ arrive?	**När avgår vi/är vi framme?** *nair afv·goar vee/air vee fra·mer*
Is flight…delayed?	**Är det någon försening på flyg…?** *air dee noa·gohn furr·seen·ihng poa flewg…*
How late will it be?	**Hur försenat är det?** *heur furr·seen·at air dee*

Luggage

Where is/are…?	**Var finns…?** *vahr fihns…*
the luggage carts [trolleys]	**bagagekärrorna** *ba·goash·chair·ohr·na*
the luggage lockers	**förvaringsskåpen** *furr·vah·rihng·skoap·ehn*
the baggage claim	**bagageutlämningen** *ba·goash·eut·lehm·nihng·ehn*
I've lost my baggage.	**Jag har förlorat mitt bagage.** *yahg hahr furr·loa·rat miht ba·goash*
My baggage has been stolen.	**Mitt bagage har blivit stulet.** *miht ba·goash hahr blee·viht steu·leht*
My suitcase was damaged.	**Min resväska blev skadad.** *Mihn rees·vehs·ka bleev skah·dad*

Finding your Way

Where is…?	**Var finns…?** *vahr fihns…*
the currency exchange office	**växelkontoret** *vehx·ehl·kohn·toar·eht*
the car hire	**biluthyrningen** *beel·eut·hewr·nihng·ehn*
the exit	**utgången** *eut·goang·ehn*
the taxi	**taxin** *tax·een*
Is there…into town?	**Finns det…in till stan?** *fihns dee… ihn tihl stahn*
a bus	**en buss** *ehn buhs*
a train	**ett tåg** *eht toag*
a subway	**tunnelbana** *tuh·nehl·bah·na*

For Asking Directions, see page 35.

YOU MAY SEE...

PLATTFORM	platform
SPÅR	tracks
INFORMATION	information
BILJETTKONTOR	ticket office
ANKOMST	arrival
AVGÅNG	departure

Train

How do I get to the train station?	**Hur kommer jag till järnvägsstationen?** *heur koh·mehr yahg tihl yairn·vaigs·sta·shoa·nehn*
How far is it?	**Hur långt är det?** *heur loangt air dee*
Where is/are...?	**Var finns...?** *vahr fihns...*
the ticket office	**biljettkontoret** *bihl·yet·kohn·toar·eht*
the luggage lockers	**förvaringsskåpen** *furr·vah·rihng·skoap·ehn*
the platforms	**plattformarna** *plat·fohr·mar·na*
Could I have a schedule [timetable], please?	**Kan jag få en tidtabell, tack?** *kan yahg foa ehn teed·ta·behl tak*
How long is the trip?	**Hur lång tid tar resan?** *heur loang teed tahr ree·san*
Is it a direct train?	**Är det ett direkttåg?** *air deh·ta eht dihr·ekt·toag*
Do I have to change trains?	**Behöver jag byta tåg?** *beh·hur·vehr yahg bew·ta toag*
Is the train on time?	**Är tåget i tid?** *air toag·het ee tihd*

For Asking Directions, see page 35.

Departures

Which platform does the train to...leave from?	**Vilken plattform går tåget till...från?** *Vihl·kehn plat·fohrm goar tao·geht froan*
When is the train to...?	**När går tåget till...?** *nair goar toa·geht tihl...*

Statens järnvägar or **SJ** (the Swedish State Railway) operates an extensive network covering the entire country, while also offering international connections to Oslo, Copenhagen and Berlin. The X2000 train, which reaches speeds up to 200 km/h, serves many of Sweden's greater cities and towns. Long-distance trains have restaurant cars and/or buffets, and there are also sleepers and couchettes for both first and second class. The system is reliable and comfortable, and offers a wide range of travel options with respect to schedule and cost. Discount tickets are available for young children, families, students and senior citizens. Special travel cards and programs are also available. On some trains, marked **R** or **IC**, you must reserve a seat by purchasing a **sittplatsbiljett** in addition to your travel ticket. For extraordinary scenery, try the northern **Inlandsbanan** (Inland Railway) service, which runs from Mora in Dalarna to Gällivare beyond the Arctic circle. The **Vildmarksexpressen** (Wilderness Express) has old 1930s coaches and a gourmet restaurant, and runs on the same line between Östersund and Gällivare, with stops and excursions.

Is this the right platform for...?	**Är det här rätta plattformen till...?** *air dee hair reh·ta plat·fohr·mehn tihl...*
Where is platform...?	**Var är plattform...?** *vahr air plat·fohrm...*
Where do I change for...?	**Var måste jag byta till...?** *vahr mos·ter yahg bew·ta tihl...*

On Board

Can I sit here/open the window?	**Kan jag sitta här/öppna fönstret?** *Kan yahg sihta hair/urp·na fuhns·streht*
Is this seat taken?	**Är den här platsen upptagen?** *air dehn hair plats·ehn uhp·tah·gehn*
That's my seat.	**Det där är min plats.** *dee dair air mihn plats*
Here's my reservation	**Här är min bokning** *Hair air meen boak·nihng*

Bus

| Where's the bus station? | **Var är bussterminalen?** *vahr air bus·tehr·mih·nahl·ehn* |

YOU MAY HEAR...

Påstigning! *poa·steeg·nihng* — All aboard!
Biljetter, tack. *bihl·yet·er tak* — Tickets, please.
Du måste byta i... *deu moss·ter bew·ta ee...* — You have to change in...
Nästa hållplats... *nehs·ta hoal·plats...* — Next stop...

YOU MAY SEE...

BUSSHÅLLPLATS bus stop
INGÅNG/UTGÅNG enter/exit
STÄMPLA ER BILJETT stamp your ticket

Public transportation in Sweden is an excellent and well-maintained system that includes **bussar** (buses), **tunnelbanan** (subways), **spårvagnar** (trams) and **tåg** (trains). All of these run frequently, usually between 5:00 a.m. and midnight on weekdays and a bit later on weekends. Most cities and towns have a bus system, though only a few have trams and subways. While it is possible to purchase single tickets for the different modes of public transportation, it is more cost efficient to purchase a card or set of tickets if you are going to be using a particular network frequently. Most major cities have websites that provide up to date information on routes, tickets and prices; many of the sites have English as a language option.

How far is it?	**Hur långt är det?** *heur loangt air dee*
How do I get to…?	**Hur kommer jag till…?** *heur koh·mehr yahg tihl…*
Does the bus stop at…?	**Stannar bussen vid…?** *stan·ar buhs·en veed…*
Could you tell me when to get off?	**Kan du tala om för mig när jag ska stiga av?** *kan deu tah·la ohm furr may nair yahg skah stee·ga afv*
Do I have to change buses?	**Behöver jag byta buss?** *beh·hur·vehr yahg bew·ta buhs*
Stop here, please.	**Stanna här, tack.** *sta·na hair tak*

For Tickets, see page 21.

Subway

Where's the nearest subway [underground] station?	**Var är närmaste tunnelbanestation?** *Vahr air nair·mas·ter tuh·nehl·bah·neh·sta·shoan*
Which direction?	**Åt vilket håll?** *Oat vihl·keht hohl*

The subway in Stockholm is efficient and easy to use. It runs from 5:00 a.m. to midnight on weekdays. Tickets are valid for one hour from the time they are stamped and can be bought from ticket booths; discount cards can be purchased from **Pressbyrån** (a newsstand). Tickets can also be purchased at **SL Centers**, some tourist offices and certain grocery stores. The public transportation websites will have information on these retailers and businesses and what types of tickets they sell. Day and multi-day cards are also available. Subway and bus tickets in Stockholm are interchangeable.

Can I have a map of the subway [underground], please?	**Kan jag få en tunnelbanekarta, tack?** *Kan yahg foa ehn tuh•nehl•bah•neh•kahr•ta tak*
Which line should I take for…?	**Vilken linje ska jag ta till…?** *vihl•kehn leen•yeh skah yahg tah tihl…*
Where do I change for…?	**Var måste jag byta till…?** *vahr mos•ter yahg bew•ta tihl…*
Is this the train to…?	**Är det här tåget till…?** *air dee hair toa•geht tihl…*
How many stops to…?	**Hur många hållplatser är det till…?** *Heur moh•ngah hohl•plat•sehr air deht tihl…*
Where are we?	**Var är vi?** *vahr air vee*

For Tickets, see page 21.

YOU MAY SEE…

LIVBÅT	life boat
FLYTVÄST	life jacket
ACTIVERA HANDBROMSEN	use parking brake
LÄMNA INTE VÄRDESAKER I BILEN	do not leave valuables in your car

Boat & Ferry

When is the car ferry to Gotland leaving?	**Hur dags går bilfärjan till Gotland?** *heur daks goar beel·fair·yan tihl goht·land*
Where are the life jackets?	**Var finns flytvästarna?** *vahr fihns flewt·vehs·tar·na*
Can I take my car?	**Kan jag ta med min bil?** *Kahn yahg tah mehd meen bihl*
Can I drive on to the ferry now?	**Får jag köra ombord nu?** *foar yahg chur·ra ohm bohrd neu*
What time is the next sailing?	**Hur dags går nästa?** *Heur daks goar nehs·ta*
Can I book a seat/cabin?	**Kan jag boka en plats/hytt?** *Kahn yahg boa·ka plats/hewt*
How long is the trip?	**Hur lång är resan?** *heur loang air ree·san*
Where should I park?	**Var ska jag parkera?** *vahr skah yahg par·kee·ra*

Taxi

| Where can I get a taxi? | **Var kan jag få tag på en taxi?** *vahr kan yahg foa tahg poa ehn tax·ee* |
| I'd like a taxi now/for tomorrow at... | **Jag skulle vilja ha en taxi nu/imorgon klockan...** *yahg skuh·ler vihl·ya hah ehn tax·ee neu/ ee·mo·ron kloh·kan...* |

Regular boat and ferry services, carrying cars and passengers, link Sweden to neighboring countries such as Norway, Denmark and Germany as well as to the U.K. Ferry services from Stockholm to the vacation destinations of Åland and Gotland in the Baltic Sea are very popular, as are ferries to Finland, Estonia and Latvia. Not to be missed are the ferry and steamer trips from Stockholm to the many surrounding islands, known as **Skärgården** (the Archipelago).

Taxis can be found at stands marked **Taxi.** You can also flag down a taxi in the street, especially near hotels and bus and train stations. Calling a taxi by phone is a third option; numbers are available from your concierge or a local phone book. The sign **Ledig** (free), when lit, indicates that the taxi is available.

Can you send a taxi?	**Kan du skicka en taxi?** *Kahn deu shih•ka ehn tax•ee*
Do you have the number for a taxi?	**Har du numret till taxi?** *Hahr deu nuhm•reht tihl tax•ee*
Pick me up at… (place/time)	**Hämta mig vid/klockan…** *hehm•ta may veed/kloh•kan…*
I'm going to…	**Jag ska resa till…** *yahg skah ree•sa tihl…*
this address	**denna adress** *deh•na ad•rehs*
the airport	**flygplatsen** *flewg•plat•sehn*
the train station	**järnvägsstationen** *yairn•vaigs•sta•shoa•nehn*
I'm late.	**Jag är sen.** *yahg air seen*
Can you drive faster/ slower?	**Kan du köra fortare/långsammare?** *Kan deu chur•ra fohrt•a•rer/loang•sam•a•rer*
Stop/Wait here.	**Stanna/Vänta här.** *sta•na/vehn•ta hair*
How much?	**Hur mycket kostar det?** *heur mew•ker kos•tar dee*
You said it would cost…kronor.	**Du sa att det skulle kosta…kronor.** *deu sah at dee skuh•ler kos•ta…kroa•nohr*
Keep the change.	**Behåll växeln.** *be•hoal vehx•ehln*
A receipt, please.	**Kvittot, tack.** *kvih•tot tak*

YOU MAY HEAR…

Vart vill du åka? *vart vihl deu oa•ka*	Where to?
Vilken adress? *vihl•kehn ad•rehs*	What's the address?

Bicycle & Motorbike

I'd like to hire…	**Jag skulle vilja hyra…** *yahg skuh•ler vihl•ya hew•ra…*
a bicycle	**en cykel** *ehn sew•kehl*
a moped	**en moped** *ehn moh•peed*
a motorbike	**en motorcykel** *ehn moa•tohr•sew•kehl*
How much per day/ week?	**Hur mycket kostar det per dag/vecka?** *heur mew•ker kos•tar dee pair dahg/veh•ka*
Can I have a helmet/ lock?	**Kan jag få en hjälm/ett cykellås?** *kan yahg foa ehn yehlm/eht sew•kehl•loas*

YOU MAY HEAR…

Har du ett internationellt körkort? *hahr deu eht in•tehr•na•shoa•nehlt churr•koart*	Do you have an international driver's license?
Kan jag få se ert pass, tack? *kan yahg foa see eert pas tak*	May I see your passport, please?
Vill du ha en försäkring? *vil deu hah ehn furr•sair•krihng*	Do you want insurance?
Det blir en handpenning på… *dee bleer ehn hand•peh•nihng poa…*	There is a deposit of…
Underteckna här, tack. *uhn•der•tehk•na hair tak*	Please sign here.

Car Hire

Where can I hire a car?	**Var kan jag hyra en bil?** *vahr kan yahg hew•ra ehn beel*
I'd like to hire…	**Jag skulle vilja hyra…** *yahg skuh•ler vihl•ya hew•ra…*
a cheap/small car	**en billig/liten bil** *en bihl•eeg/lee•tehn beel*
a 2-/4-door car	**en bil med två/fyra dörrar** *ehn beel meed tvoa/few•ra dur•rar*

an automatic/ manual car	**en bil med automatväxel/ manuell** *ehn beel meed ah•toa•maht•vehx•ehl/ mah•nuh•ehl*
a car with air-conditioning	**en bil med luftkonditionering** *ehn beel meed luhft•kohn•dee•shoa•neer•ihng*
a car seat	**en bilbarnstol** *ehn beel•barn•stoal*
How much does it cost…?	**Hur mycket kostar det…?** *heur mew•ker kos•tar dee…*
per day/week	**per dag/vecka** *pair dahg/veh•ka*
per kilometer	**per kilometer** *pair chee•loh•mee•ter*
How much does it cost…?	**Hur mycket kostar det…?** *heur mew•ker kos•tar dee…*
for unlimited mileage	**för obegränsade mil** *furr oa•beh•grehn•sa•deh•meel*
with insurance	**med försäkring** *meed furr•sair•krihng*
Are there any special weekend rates?	**Har ni särskilda helgrabatter?** *hahr nee sair•shihl•da hely•ra•bat•ehr*

Fuel Station

Where's the next fuel station, please?	**Ursäkta, var är närmaste bensinstation?** *eur•shehk•ta vahr air nair•mas•the behn•seen•sta•shoar*
Fill it up, please.	**Fyll tanken, tack.** *feyl tan•kehn tak*
…liters, please.	**…liter, tack….** *lee•tehr tak*
I'll pay in cash/by credit card.	**Jag betalar kontant/med kreditkort.** *Yahg beh•tah•lar kohn•tant/meed kreh•deet•koart*

YOU MAY SEE…

VANLIG	regular
PREMIUM	premium [super]
DIESEL	diesel

Asking Directions

Is this the road to…?	**Är det här vägen till…?**	*air dee hair vair·gehn tihl…*
How far is it to…?	**Hur långt är det till…?**	*heur loangt air dee tihl…*
Where's…?	**Var ligger…?**	*vahr lih·gehr…*
…Street	**…gata**	*…gah·ta*
this address	**denna adress**	*deh·na ad·rehs*
the highway [motorway]	**motorvägen**	*moa·tohr·vair·gehn*
Can you show me on the map?	**Kan du visa mig på kartan?**	*kan deu vee·sa may poa kahr·tan*
I'm lost.	**Jag har kommit vilse.**	*yahg hahr koh·miht vihl·ser*

YOU MAY HEAR…

rakt fram *rahkt fram*	straight ahead
till vänster *tihl vehn·stehr*	on/to the left
till höger *tihl hur·gehr*	on/to the right
i/runt hörnan *ee/ruhnt hur·nan*	on/around the corner
mitt emot *miht ee·moat*	opposite
bakom *bah·kohm*	behind
bredvid *breh·veed*	next to
efter *ehf·tehr*	after
norr/söder *nohr/sur·dehr*	north/south
öster/väster *urs·tehr/vehs·tehr*	east/west
vid trafikljusen *veed tra·feek·yeus·ehn*	at the traffic light
vid avfarten *veed afv·far·tehn*	at the exit

YOU MAY SEE...

	STOPP	stop
	LÄMNA FÖRETRÄDE	yield
	PARKERING FÖRBJUDEN	no parking
	FARLIG KURVA	dangerous curve
	ENKELRIKTAT	one way
	INGEN INFART	no entry
	OMKÖRNING FÖRBJUDEN	no passing
	U-SVÄNG FÖRBJUDEN	no U-turn
	ÖVERGÅNGSSTÄLLE FÖR FOTGÄNGARE	pedestrian crossing

Parking

Can I park here?	**Får jag parkera här?** *foar yahg par‑kee‑ra hair*	
Is there a parking lot [car park] nearby?	**Finns det en parkeringsplats i närheten?** *fihns dee ehn par‑kee‑rihngs‑plats ee närhee‑tehn*	
Where's...?	**Var ligger...?** *Vahr lih‑gehr...*	
the parking garage	**parkeringshuset** *par‑kee‑rihngs‑huhseht*	
the parking meter	**parkeringsautomaten** *par‑kee‑rihngs ah‑toa‑mah‑tehn*	
How much does it cost...?	**Hur mycket koster det...?** *heur mew‑ker kos‑tar dee...*	

per hour	**per timme** *pair tihm·er*
per day	**per dag** *pair dahg*
overnight	**över natten** *ur·vehr na·tehn*

Breakdown & Repair

My car broke down/ won't start.	**Min bil har gått sönder/startar inte.** *min beel hahr goat sun·dehr/star·tar in·ter*
Can you fix it today?	**Kan ni laga den idag?** *kan nee lah·ga dehn ee·dahg*
When will it be ready?	**När blir den färdig?** *nair bleer dehn fair·dihg*
How much?	**Hur mycket kostar det?** *heur mew·ker kos·tar dee*
I have a puncture/ flat tyre (tire)	**Jag har punktering** *Yahg hahr puhng·teh·rihng*

Street parking, parking lots and, in some cases, parking garages will be available in most of Sweden's cities and larger towns. Street parking is generally metered in city centers and downtown areas. A blue circular sign with a red slash tells you where parking is prohibited. There will be signs indicating whether or not parking is free. In places where parking is metered, a ticket allowing you to park for a specific period of time will need to be purchased. If this is the case, tickets can be purchased from a **biljettautomat** (ticket machine). You pay for the amount of time you want to park and then place the ticket on the driver's side of the car, on the dashboard, so that the ticket is in plain sight. In some cases, parking may be free, and there will be signs posted with time limits, usually two or three hours.

Accidents

| There's been an accident | **Det har hänt en olycka.** *dee hahr hehnt ehn oa·lew·ka* |
| Call an ambulance/ the police. | **Ring efter en ambulans/polisen.** *rihng ehf·ter ehn am·beu·lans/poa·lee·sehn* |

Places to Stay

ESSENTIAL

Can you recommend a hotel in…? **Kan du rekommendera ett hotel i…?** *kan deu reh‑koh‑mehn‑dee‑ra eht hoh‑tehl ee…*

I have a reservation. **Jag har bokat rum.** *yahg hahr boa‑kat ruhm*

My name is… **Jag heter…** *yahg hee‑tehr…*

Do you have a room…? **Har ni ett ledigt rum…?** *hahr nee eht lee‑dihgt ruhm…*

for one/two **för en person/två personer** *furr ehn pehr‑shoan/tvoa pehr‑shoan‑ehr*

with a bathroom **med badrum** *meed bahd‑ruhm*

with air‑conditioning **med luftkonditionering** *meed luhft‑kohn‑dee‑shoa‑neer‑ihng*

For tonight. **För ikväll.** *furr ee‑kvehl*

For two nights. **För två nätter.** *furr tvoa neh‑tehr*

For one week. **För en vecka.** *furr ehn veh‑ka*

How much? **Hur mycket kostar det?** *heur mew‑ker kos‑tar dee*

Do you have anything cheaper? **Har ni någonting billigare?** *hahr nee noa‑gohn‑tihng bihl‑ee‑ga‑rer*

When's check‑out? **När måste vi checka ut?** *nair mos‑ter vee sheh‑ka eut*

Can I leave this in the safe? **Kan jag lämna detta i kassaskåpet?** *Kan yahg lehm‑na deh‑ta ee ka‑sah‑skoa‑peht*

Could we leave our baggage here until…? **Kan vi lämna vårt bagage här till klockan…?** *kan vee lehm‑na voart ba‑goash hair tihl kloh‑kan…*

Could I have the bill/receipt, please? **Kan jag få räkningen/kvittot, tack?** *Kan yahg foa rairk‑nihng‑en/kvih‑toht tak*

I'll pay in cash/by credit card. **Jag betalar kontant/med kreditkort.** *Yahg beh‑tah‑lar kohn‑tant/meed kreh‑deet‑koart*

38

Somewhere to Stay

Can you recommend a hotel in…?	**Kan du rekommendera ett hotel i…?** *kan deu reh·koh·mehn·dee·ra eht hoh·tehl ee…*
a hostel	**ett vandrarhem** *eht vand·rar·hehm*
a campsite	**en kampingplats** *ehn kam·pihng·plats*
a bed and breakfast	**rum med frukost** *ruhm mehd fruh·kohst*
What is it near?	**Vad finns det i närheten?** *vahd fihns dee ee nair·hee·tehn*
How do I get there?	**Hur kommer jag dit?** *heur koh·mehr yahg deet*

At the Hotel

I have a reservation.	**Jag har bokat rum.** *yahg hahr boh·kat ruhm*
My name is…	**Jag heter…** *yahg hee·tehr…*
Do you have a room…?	**Har ni ett rum…?** *hahr nee eht ruhm…*
with a bathroom/shower	**med bad/dusch** *meed bahd/deush*
with air conditioning	**med luftkonditionering** *meed luhft·kohn·dee·shoa·neer·ihng*
that's smoking/non-smoking	**för rökare/icke-rökare** *furr rur·kah·rer/ih·keh rur·ka·rer*
For tonight.	**För ikväll.** *furr ee·kvehl*

For two nights.	**För två nätter.** *furr tvoa neh·tehr*
For one week.	**För en vecka.** *furr ehn veh·ka*
Does the hotel have...?	**Finns det...på hotellet?** *fihns dee...poa hoh·tehl·eht*
a computer	**en dator** *ehn dah·tohr*
an elevator [lift]	**en hiss** *ehn hihs*
(wireless) internet service	**(trådlös) internet** *(troad·lurs) in·tehr·net*
room service	**rumservice** *ruhm·sehr·vihs*
a pool	**en simbassäng** *ehn sihm·ba·sehng*
a gym	**ett gym** *eht ym*
I need...	**Jag behöver...** *yahg beh·hur·vehr...*
an extra bed	**en extra säng** *ehn ehx·tra sehng*
a cot	**en tältsäng** *ehn tehlt·sehng*
a crib	**en barnsäng** *ehn bahrn·sehng*

For Numbers, see page 179.

YOU MAY HEAR...

Ert pass/kreditkort, tack. *ehrt pas/ kreh·deet·koart tak*	Your passport/credit card, please.
Kan du fylla i den här blanketten. *kan deu few·la ee dehn hair blan·keh·tehn*	Please fill out this form.
Skriv under här. *skreev uhn·der hair*	Sign here.

Price

| How much per night/week? | **Vad kostar det per natt/vecka?** *Vahd kos·tar dee pair nat/veh·ka* |

| Does the price include breakfast/sales tax [VAT]? | **Ingår frukost/moms i priset?** _ihn•**goar** fruh•kohst/mohms ee **pree**•seht_ |
| Are there any discounts? | **Ger ni rabatter?** _Yehr nee ra•bat•ehr_ |

There is a wide range of places to stay in Sweden, from luxury to budget. Budget options include **privatrum** (private rooms), much like bed and breakfasts, or **stugor** (cabins) and **lägenheter** (apartments). Cabins and apartments are usually rented out on a weekly basis, but one- or two-night stays may also be an option. Information can be found at the local tourist office; you may also see signs along the road indicating that there is a vacancy in a cabin nearby. Motorists can look for **motel** (motels); these are reasonably priced with restaurants and car-friendly facilities. When looking for somewhere to stay in university towns such as Stockholm, Göteborg or Lund, staying at a **sommarhotel** (summer hotel) can be a good choice. Student dormitories are open to tourists in the summer and are a good option if you are traveling in a group. Families can enjoy a **familjehotell** (a family hotel), which has special rates for groups sharing the same room (three to six beds). These only operate during the summer months. All-inclusive accommodation is also available in the form of a **turisthotell** (tourist hotel) or **pensionat** (boarding house). These are clean and comfortable hotels or guesthouses that are often found at summer resorts and winter sport areas. Sweden also offers first class and deluxe hotels, usually found in larger cities and towns. Prices and amenities vary but the standards are usually high. Breakfast is usually included. When booking somewhere to stay during the summer months and high tourist season it is important to book in advance.

Preferences

Can I see the room?	**Kan jag se rummet?**	*Kan yahg seh ruhm·eht*
I'd like a...room.	**Jag skulle vilja ha ett...rum.**	*Yahg skuh·ler vihl·ya hah eht ...ruhm*
better	**bättre** *beh·treh*	
bigger	**större** *stuh·reh*	
cheaper	**billigare** *bihl·ee·ga·rer*	
quieter	**tystare** *tews·tah·rer*	
I'll take it.	**Ja tar det.** *Yahg tahr deht*	
No, I won't take it.	**Nej, jag tar inte det.** *Nay, yahg tahr deht in·ter*	

Questions

Where's...?	**Var ligger...?**	*vahr <u>lih</u>·gehr...*
the bar	**baren** <u>*bah*</u>·*rehn*	
the bathroom [toilet]	**toaletten** *toa·ah·<u>leh</u>·tehn*	
the elevator [lift]	**hissen** <u>*his*</u>·*ehn*	
Can I have...?	**Kan jag få...?** *kan yahg foa...*	
a blanket	**ett täcke** *eht <u>teh</u>·ker*	
an iron	**ett strykjärn** *eht <u>strewk</u>·yairn*	
the room key/ key card	**rumsnyckeln/nyckelkortet** *Ruhms·new·kehl/ new·kehl·koart*	
a pillow	**en kudde** *ehn <u>keu</u>·der*	
soap	**tvål** *tvoal*	
toilet paper	**toalettpapper** *toa·ah·<u>leht</u>·pa·pehr*	
a towel	**en handduk** *ehn <u>han</u>·d**euk***	
Can I use this adapter here?	**Kan jag använda den här adaptern här?** *kan yahg <u>an</u>·vehn·da dehn hair a·<u>dap</u>·tern hair*	
How do I turn on the lights?	**Hur tänder man lamporna?** *heur <u>tehn</u>·der man <u>lam</u>·pohr·na*	

YOU MAY SEE...

TRYCK	push
DRAG	pull
WC	restroom [toilet]
DAMTOALETT	women's restroom
HERRTOALETT	men's restroom
DUSCH	shower
HISS	elevator [lift]
TRAPPOR	stairs
TVÄTT	laundry
VAR GOD STÖR EJ	do not disturb
BRANDUTGÅNG	fire door
NÖDUTGÅNG	emergency exit
TELEFONVÄCKNING	wake-up call

Could you wake me at…?	**Kan ni väcka mig klockan…?** *kan nee veh•ka may kloh•kan…*
Could I have my things from the safe?	**Kan jag få mina saker från kassaskåpet?** *kan yahg foa mee•na sah•ker froan ka•sa•skoa•peht*
Is there any mail/a message for me?	**Finns det någon post/eht meddelande till mig?** *fihns dee noa•gohn pohst/eht meed•deel•an•der tihl may*
Do you have a laundry service?	**Har ni tvättservice?** *hahr nee tveht•sehr•vihs*

Problems

There's a problem.	**Jag har ett problem.** *yahg hahr eht proh•bleem*
I've lost my key/ key card.	**Jag har tappat bort min nyckel/mitt nyckelkort.** *yahg hahr ta•pat bort mihn new•kehl/ miht new•kehl•koart*

Throughout Sweden the current is 230-volt, 50-cycle AC. If you bring your own electrical appliances, buy a continental adapter plug (round pins) before leaving home. You may also need a transformer appropriate to the wattage of the appliance.

I've locked myself out of my room.	**Jag har låst ut mig ur rummet.** *yahg hahr loast eut may eur ruhm•eht*
There's no hot water/toilet paper.	**Det finns inget varmvatten/toalettpapper.** *dee fihns ihng•eht varmt•va•tehrn/toa•ah•leht•pa•per*
The room is dirty.	**Rummet är smutsigt.** *ruhm•eht air smuht•siht*
There are bugs in our room.	**Det finns insekter på vårt rum.** *dee fihns ihn•sehk•tehr poa voart ruhm*
Can you fix…?	**Kan ni laga…?** *kan nee lah•ga…*
the air conditioning	**luftkonditioneringen** *luhft•kohn•dee•shoa•neer•ihng•ehn*
the fan	**fläkten** *flehk•tehn*
the heating	**värmen** *vair•mehn*
the light	**lampan** *lahm•pan*
the TV	**teven** *teh•veen*
the toilet	**toaletten** *toa•ah•leh•tehn*
I'd like to move to another room.	**Jag skulle vilja flytta till ett annat rum.** *yahg skuh•ler vihl•ya flew•ta tihl eht an•at ruhm*
…is/are broken.	**…är trasig.** *…air trah•sihg*

Checking Out

When do we need to check out?	**När måste vi checka ut?** *nair mos•ter vee sheh•ka eut*
Could we leave our	**Kan vi lämna vårt bagage här till**

baggage here until...?	**klockan...?** *kan vee <u>lehm</u>•na voart ba•<u>goash</u> hair tihl <u>kloh</u>•kan...*
Can I have an itemized bill/receipt?	**Kan jag få en specificerad räkning/ ett specificerad kvitto?** *kan yahg foa ehn <u>speh</u>•seh•fee•<u>ee</u>•rad rairk•ning/eht <u>speh</u>•seh•fee•<u>ee</u>•rad <u>kvih</u>•toh*
I think there's a mistake in this bill.	**Jag tror det måste vara fel på notan.** *Yahg troar dee <u>mos</u>•ter <u>vah</u>•ra feel poa <u>noa</u>•tan.*
I'll pay in cash/by credit card.	**Jag betalar kontant/med kreditkort.** *Yahg beh•<u>tah</u>•lar kohn•<u>tant</u>/meed kreh•<u>deet</u>•koart*

Renting

I've reserved an apartment/a room.	**Jag har bokat en lägenhet/ett rum.** *Yahg hahr <u>boh</u>•kat ehn <u>lair</u>•gehn•h<u>eet</u>/eht ruhm*
My name is...	**Jag heter...** *yahg <u>hee</u>•tehr...*
Can I have the key/ key card?	**Kan jag få nyckeln/nyckelkortet?** *kan yahg foa <u>new</u>•kehln/<u>new</u>•kehl•<u>koar</u>•teht*
Are there...?	**Finns det...?** *fihns dee...*
dishes	**porslin** *poarsh•<u>leen</u>*
pillows	**kuddar** <u>keu</u>•dar
sheets	**lakan** <u>lah</u>•kan
towels	**handdukar** han•d<u>eu</u>•kar

A service charge as well as **moms** (sales tax) is included in hotel and restaurant bills, but you are expected to round up a restaurant bill to the nearest **krona**. Tipping is generally not expected, but it's always appreciated if the service has been exceptionally good. It is customary to give a small tip to hairdressers, barbers, taxi drivers and porters.

45

utensils	**bestick** beh·_stihk_
When do I put out the bins/recycling?	**När ska jag ställa ut soporna/ återvinning?** nair skah yahg _steh_·la eut _soa_·pohr·na/ oat·ehr·vihn·ing
...has broken down.	**...har gått sönder.** ... hahr goat _surn_·dehr
How does...work?	**Hur fungerar...?** heur fuhn·_geh_·rar...
the air-conditioner	**luftkonditioneringen** _luhft_·kohn·dee·shoa·_neer_·ihng·ehn
the dishwasher	**diskmaskinen** dihsk·ma·_shee_·nehn
the freezer	**frysen** _frew_·sen
the heater	**värmeelementet** _vair_·meh·ehl·eh·_mehn_·teht
the microwave	**mikrovågsugnen** mik·roh·_voags_·_eung_·nehn
How does...work?	**Hur fungerar...?** heur fuhn·_geh_·rar...
the refrigerator	**kylskåpet** kewl·_skoa_·peht
the stove	**spisen** _spee_·sehn
the washing machine	**tvättmaskinen** tveht·mah·_shee_·nehn

Domestic Items

I'd like...	**Jag skulle vilja ha...** yahg _skuh_·ler _vihl_·ya hah...
an adapter	**en adapter** ehn a·_dap_·tehr
aluminum	**aluminiumfolie** ah·leu·_mee_·nee·um·foh·lyer foil
a bottle opener	**en flasköppnare** ehn flask·_urp_·na·rer
a broom	**en sopborste** ehn sop·borsh·ter
a can opener	**en konservöppnare** ehn kohn·_serv_·urp·na·rer
cleaning supplies	**städutrustning** staird·_eut_·reust·nihng
a corkscrew	**en korkskruv** ehn _kohrk_·skreuv
detergent	**tvättmedel** _tveht_·mee·dehl
dishwashing liquid	**diskmedel** _disk_·mee·dehl
bin bags	**soppåsar** _sop_·poa·sar
a light bulb	**en glödlampa** ehn _glurd_·lam·pa
matches	**tändstickor** _tehnd_·stih·kohr

a mop	**en skurmopp** *ehn skewr·mop*
napkins	**pappersservetter** *pa·pers·sahr·veh·ter*
plastic wrap	**plastfolie** *plast·foh·lyer*
[cling film]	
a plunger	**en vaskrensare** *ehn vask·rehn·sa·rer*
scissors	**en sax** *ehn sax*
a vacuum cleaner	**en dammsugare** *ehn damm·seu·ga·rer*

For In the Kitchen, see page 83.

For Oven Temperatures, see page 186.

At the Hostel

Do you have any places left for tonight?	**Finns det några lediga platser ikväll?** *fihns dee noa·gra lee·dih·ga plats·ehr ee·kvehl*
Can I have…?	**Kan jag få…?** *kan yahg foa…*
a single/double room	**ett enkelrum/dubbelrum** *eht hng·kehl·ruhm/duh·behl·ruhm*
a blanket	**ett täcke** *eht tehk·er*
a pillow	**en kudde** *ehn keu·der*

If you are looking for something comfortable and reasonably priced, **Svenska Turistföreningen** or **STF** (the Swedish Tourist Club) is an excellent place to start. Here you can search for accommodations such as **vandrarhem** (youth hostels). If you are a member of **STF** or Hostelling International you get a member discount. Generally, room options include dormitory style rooms, split male and female, as well as smaller private rooms or family rooms. You are usually expected to bring your own towels and sheets as these usually are not provided, but can be rented. Shared kitchen facilities are often available, so that you can buy food at the local supermarket and prepare your own meals. Some hostels offer breakfast.

sheets	**lakan** _lah_·kan
a towel	**en handduk** ehn _han_·deuk
What time are the doors locked?	**När stängs ytterdörrarna?** nair stehngs _ew_·ter·dur·ar·na
Do I need a membership card?	**Behöver jag medlemskort?** beh·hur·vehr yahg mehd·lehms·koart
Here's my international student card.	**Här är mitt internationella studentkort.** hair air miht in·tehr·na·shoa·nehl·ah stuh·dehnt·koart

Going Camping

Can I camp here?	**Får man tälta här?** foar man _tehl_·ta hair
Is there a campsite near here?	**Finns det en campingplats i närheten?** fihns dee ehn _kam_·pihng·plats ee _nair_·hee·tehn
What is the charge per day/week?	**Vad kostar det per dag/vecka?** vahd _kos_·tar dee pair dahg/_veh_·ka
Are there…?	**Finns det…?** fihns dee…
cooking facilities	**kokmöjligheter** _koak_·mury·lihg·hee·tehr
electrical outlets	**nätuttag** _nairt_·eut·tahg
laundry facilities	**tvättmöjligheter** _tveht_·mury·lig·hee·tehr
showers	**dusch** deush
tents for hire	**tält för uthyrning** tehlt furr _eut_·hewr·nihng
Where can I empty the chemical toilet?	**Var kan jag tömma den kemiska toaletten?** vahr kan yahg _tur_·ma dehn _sheh_·mihs·ka toa·ah·_leh_·tehn

For Domestic Items, see page 46.

YOU MAY SEE…

DRICKSVATTEN	drinking water
INGEN CAMPING	no camping
INGEN GRILLNING	no barbeques
INGEN ÖPPEN ELD	no fires

Communications

ESSENTIAL

Where's an internet cafe?	**Var finns det ett internetkafé?** *vahr fihns dee eht ihn•tehr•neht•ka•feh*
Can I access the internet/check e-mail here?	**Kan jag komma ut på internet/kola e-post här?** *kan yahg koh•ma eut poa ihn•tehr•neht/koa•la ee•pohst hair*
How much per hour/half hour?	**Hur mycket kostar det per timme/halvtimme?** *heur mew•ker kos•tar dee pair tihm•er/halv•tihm•er*
How do I connect/log on?	**Hur loggar jag in?** *heur loh•gar yag ihn*
Can I have a phone card?	**Kan jag få ett telefonkort?** *kan yahg foa eht teh•leh•foan•koart*
Can I have your phone number?	**Kan jag få ditt telefonnummer?** *kan yahg foa diht teh•leh•foan•nuhm•ehr*
Here's my number/e-mail address.	**Här är mitt nummer/min e-postadress.** *hair air miht nuhm•ehr/mihn ee•pohst•ad•rehs*
Call me.	**Var snäll och ring mig.** *vahr snehl ohk ring may*
E-mail me.	**Skicka en e-post till mig.** *shih•ka ehn ee•pohst tihl may*
Hello. This is…	**Hej. Det här är…** *hay dee hair air…*
I'd like to speak to…	**Jag skulle vilja tala med…** *yahg skuh•ler vihl•ya tah•la meed…*
Repeat that, please.	**Kan du upprepa det, tack.** *kan deu uhp•ree•pa dee tak*
I'll be in touch.	**Jag hör av mig snart.** *yahg hur afv may snahrt*
Goodbye.	**Hej då.** *hay doa*
Where is the post office?	**Var ligger posten?** *vahr lih•gehr pohs•tehn*

| I'd like to send this to... | **Jag skulle vilja skicka det här till...** |
| | *yahg skuh•ler vihl•ya shih•ka dee hair tihl...* |

Online

Where's an internet cafe?	**Var finns det ett internetcafe?** *vahr fihns deht eht ihn•tehr•neht•ka•feh*
Does it have wireless internet?	**Finns det trådlös internet där?** *fihns dee troad•lurs ihn•tehr•neht dair*
What is the WiFi password?	**Vilket är WiFi-lösenordet?** *vihl•keht wai•fai•lur•sehn•oarde*
Is the WiFi free?	**Är WiFi:n gratis?** *air wai•fain grah•tihs*
Do you have bluetooth?	**Har ni blåtand?** *hahr nee bloa•tand*
How do I turn the computer on/off?	**Hur sätter jag på/stänger jag av datorn?** *heur seh•tehr yahg poa/stehng•her yahg afv dah•torn*
Can I print?	**Kan jag skriva ut?** *kan yahg skree•va eut*
Can I...?	**Kan jag...?** *kahn yahg...*
access the internet	**gå ut på internet** *goa eut poa ihn•tehr•neth*
check my e-mail	**kolla min e-post** *kohla meen eh•pohst*
plug in/charge my laptop/iPhone/iPad/BlackBerry?	**sätta i/ladda min laptop/iPhone/iPad/BlackBerry** *sehta ih/ladha meen laptop/iPad/BlackBerry*
access Skype?	**använda Skype** *an•vehn•a Skype*
How much per half hour/hour?	**Hur mycket kostar det per halvtimme/timme?** *Heur mew•keh koh•star deht pehr halv•tihm•er/tih•mer*
How do I...?	**Hur gör man för att...?** *heur yurr man furr at...*
connect/disconnect	**koppla upp/koppla ner** *kohp•la uhp/kohp•la nehr*
log on/off	**logga in/ut** *loh•ga ihn/eut*
type this symbol	**skriva in det här tecknet** *skree•va ihn dee hair tehk•neht*

What's your e-mail?	**Vad har du för e-postadress?** *vahd hahr deu fu*rr *ee-pohst-ad-rehs*
My e-mail is...	**Min e-postadress är...** *mihn ee-pohst-ad-rehs air...*
Do you have a scanner?	**Har ni en skanner?** *Hahr nee ehn ska-nehr*

Social Media

Are you on Facebook/ Twitter?	**Finns du på Facebook/Twitter?** *Fihns deu poa Facebook/Twitter*
What's your user name?	**Vilket användarnamn har du?** *Vihl-keht an-vehn-dar-namn hahr deu*
I'll add you as a friend.	**Jag lägger till dig som vän.** *yahg lehg-ehr tihl day sohm vehn*
I'll follow you on Twitter.	**Jag följer dig på Twitter.** *Yahg fuhl-yehr day poa Twitter*
Are you following...?	**Följer du...?** *Fuhl-yehr deu...*
I'll put the pictures on Facebook/Twitter.	**Jag lägger ut bilderna på Facebook/Twitter.** *yahg lehg-ehr eut bihl-dehr-na poa Facebook/Twitter*
I'll tag you in the pictures.	**Jag taggar bilderna.** *yahg ta-gar bihl-dehr-na*

YOU MAY SEE...

STÄNG	close
RADERA	delete
E-POST	e-mail
UTGÅNG	exit
HJÄLP	help
INSTANT MESSENGER	instant messenger
INTERNET	internet
LOGGA IN	login
NYTT MEDDELANDE	new message
AV/PÅ	on/off
ÖPPNA	open
SKRIV UT	print
SPARA	save
SKICKA	send
ANVÄNDARNAMN	username
LÖSENORD	password
TRÅDLÖS INTERNET	wireless internet

Phone

A phone card/prepaid phone please.	**Ett telefonkort, tack.** *eht teh·leh·foan·koart tak*
How much does it cost?	**Hur mycket kostar det?** *heur mew·ker kos·tar dee*
What's the area/country code for…?	**Vad är riktnumret/landskoden till…?** *vahd air rikt·nuhm·reht/lands·koa·dehn tihl…*
What's the number for Information?	**Vilket nummer är det till Nummerbyrån?** *vihl·keht nuhm·ehr air dee tihl nuhm·ehr·bew·roan*
I'd like the number for…	**Jag skulle vilja ha numret till…** *yahg skuh·ler vihl·ya hah nuhm·reht tihl…*
I'd like to call collect [reverse the charges].	**Jag vill ringa ett mottagaren-betalar-samtal.** *yahg vihl rihng·a eht moh·tah·ga·ren be·tah·lar-sam·tahl*
My phone doesn't work here.	**Min telefon fungerar inte här.** *mihn teh·leh·foan fuhn·geh·rar ihn·ter hair*
What network are you on?	**Vilket nätverk använder du?** *vihl·keht neht·vehrk an·vehn·der deu*
Is it 3G?	**Är det 3G?** *air deht treh·geh*
I have run out of credit/minutes.	**Jag har inte mer pengar/minuter på kortet.** *yahg hahr ihn·ther meer pehng·ar/mih·nuh·tehr poa koart·eht*
Can I buy some credit?	**Kan jag fylla på kortet?** *kahn yahg fewlah poa koart·et*
Do you have a phone charger?	**Har du/ni en telefonladdare?** *Hahr deu/nee ehn teh·leh·foan·lad·ar·eh*
Can I have your number?	**Kan jag få ditt telefonnummer?** *kan yahg foa diht teh·leh·foan·nuhm·ehr*
Here's my number.	**Här är mitt nummer.** *hair air miht nuhm·ehr*
Please call me.	**Var snäll och ring mig.** *vahr snehl ohk rihng may*
Please text me.	**Var snäll och skicka ett sms till mig.** *Vahr snehl ohk shih·ka eht ehs·ehm·ehs tihl may*

YOU MAY HEAR...

Vem är det? *vehm air dee* — Who's calling?

Ett ögonblick. *eht ur·gohn·blihk* — One moment.

Tyvärr, är han/hon inte här. *tew·vair air hahn/hoan ihn·ter hair* — I'm afraid he/she is not in.

Han/Hon kan inte komma till telefonen. *hahn/hoan kan ihn·ter koh·ma tihl teh·leh·foan·ehn* — He/She can't come to the phone.

Vill du lämna ett meddelande? *vihl deu lehm·na eht mee·dee·lan·der* — Would you like to leave a message?

Ring tillbaka senare/om tio minuter. *rihng tihl·bah·ka see·na·rer/ohm tee·oah mih·neu·tehr* — Call back later/in 10 minutes.

Kan han/hon ringa upp dig? *kan hahn/hoan rihng·a uhp day* — Can he/she call you back?

Vad är ditt telefonnummer? *vahd air diht teh·leh·foan·nuhm·her* — What's your number?

I'll call you.	**Jag ringer dig.** *yahg rihng·ehr day*
I'll text you.	**Jag skickar ett sms till dig.** *yahg shih·kar eht ehs·ehm·ehs tihl day*

Telephone Etiquette

Hello. This is…	**Hej. Det här är…** *hay dee hair air…*
I'd like to speak to…	**Jag skulle vilja tala med…** *yahg skuh·ler vihl·ya tah·la meed…*
Extension…	**Anknytning…** *an·knewt·nihng…*
Speak louder/more slowly.	**Var snäll och tala högre/långsammare.** *vahr snehl ohk tah·la hur·greh/loang·sam·a·rer*

Can you repeat that?	**Kan du upprepa det?** *kan deu uhp•ree•pa d**ee***
I'll call back later.	**Jag ringer senare.** *yahg rihng•ehr see•na•rer*
Goodbye.	**Hej då.** *hay doa*

Fax

Can I send/receive a fax here?	**Kan man skicka/ta emot fax här?** *kan man shih•ka/ta ee•**moat** fax hair*
What's the fax number?	**Vad är ditt faxnummer?** *vahd air diht fax•nuhm•ehr*
Please fax this to…	**Var snäll och faxa det här till…** *vahr snehl ohk fax•ah d**ee** hair tihl…*

Public phones take either **telefonkort** (phone cards) or **kreditkort** (credit cards). Phone cards are available at **Pressbyrån** (newsstand chain) and sometimes at independent newsstands. You can purchase a cell phone with a prepaid SIM card, something which is relatively cost efficient and worthwhile if you will be in Sweden for a longer period. Phone cards can also be used when dialing from any landline, e.g. at home of a friend or from a hotel. To call the U.S. or Canada from Sweden, dial 00 + 1 + area code + phone number. To call the U.K., dial 00 + 44 + area code (minus first 0) + phone number. Information on area codes for Sweden and international dialing codes can be found in the phone book and are usually available at hotels and youth hostels. The emergency number in Sweden is 112.

YOU MAY HEAR...

Fyll i tulldeklarationen, tack. *fewl ee* *tuhl•deh•klar•a•shoa•nehn tak*

Please fill out the customs declaration form.

Vad är värdet? *vahd air vair•deht*

What's the value?

Vad finns inuti? *vahd fihns ihn•eu•tee*

What's inside?

Post

Where's the post office/mailbox?	**Var ligger posten/postlådan?** *vahr lih•gehr pohs•tehn/pohst•loa•dan*
A stamp for this postcard/letter, please.	**Kan jag få ett frimärke till det här vykortet/brevet, tack.** *kan yahg foa eht free•mair•ker tihl dee hair vew•koar•teht/bree•veht tak*
How much does it cost?	**Hur mycket kostar det?** *heur mew•ker kos•tar dee*
I want to send this package by airmail/express.	**Jag vill skicka det här paketet med flygpost/express.** *yahg vihl shih•ka dee hair pa•kee•teht meed flewg•pohst/ehx•prehs*
The receipt, please.	**Kvittot, tack.** *kvih•toht tak*

Posten (the post office) is easy to find, just look for the blue **Post** sign with a yellow horn. Mailboxes are bright yellow. Business hours are 9:00 a.m. to 6:00 p.m. and until 1:00 p.m. on Saturdays. Like many other stores and business, you will need to take a number and wait for it to be called or displayed on a screen before you can be helped. Stamps can be purchased at **Pressbyrån** (newsstand chain) as well as some grocery stores.

Food & Drink

Eating Out	58
Meals & Cooking	65
Drinks	84
On the Menu	89

Eating Out

ESSENTIAL

Can you recommend a good restaurant/bar?	**Kan du rekommendera en bra restaurang/pub?** kan deu reh·koh·mehn·_dee_·ra ehn brah rehs·teu·_rang_/peub
Is there a traditional Swedish/an inexpensive restaurant nearby?	**Finns det något värdshus/någon billigare restaurang i närheten?** fihns dee _noa_·goht _vairds_·heus/_noa_·gohn _bihl_·ih·ga·rer rehs·teu·_rang_ ee nair·_hee_·tehn
A table for..., please.	**Ett bord för..., tack.** eht bohrd furr...tak
Could we sit...?	**Får vi sitta...?** foar vee _siht_·a...
here/there	**här/där** hair/dair
outside	**ute** _eu_·ter
in a non-smoking area	**vid bord för icke-rökare** veed bohrd furr _ee_·keh·_rur_·ka·rer
I'm waiting for someone.	**Jag väntar på någon.** yahg _vairn_·tar poa _noa_·gohn
Where are the toilets?	**Var finns toaletten?** vahr fihns toa·ah·_leh_·tehn
A menu, please.	**En meny, tack.** ehn _meh_·neu tak
What do you recommend?	**Vad rekommenderar du?** vahd reh·koh·mehn·_dee_·rar deu
I'd like...	**Jag skulle vilja ha...** yahg _skuh_·ler _vihl_·ya hah...
Some more..., please.	**Lite mer..., tack.** _lee_·ter meer...tak
Enjoy your meal.	**Smaklig måltid.** _smahk_·lihg _moal_·teed
The check [bill], please.	**Kan jag få räkningen, tack.** kan yahg foa _rairk_·nihng·ehn tak
Is service included?	**Är serveringsavgiften inräknad?** air ser·_veeh_·rihngs·afv·_yihf_·tehn _ihn_·rairk·nad

Can I pay by credit card?	**Kan jag betala med kreditkort?** *kan yahg beh•tah•la meed kreh•deet•koart*
Can I have the receipt, please?	**Kan jag få kvittot, tack?** *kan yahg foa kvih•toht tak*
Thank you.	**Tack.** *tak*

Where to Eat

Can you recommend...?	**Kan du rekommendera...?** *kan deu reh•koh•mehn•dee•ra...*
a restaurant	**en restaurang** *ehn rehs•teu•rang*
a bar	**en bar** *ehn bahr*
a cafe	**ett kafé** *eht ka•feh*
a fast-food place	**en grillbar** *ehn grihl•bahr*
a steakhouse	**ett stekhus** *eht steek•heus*
a cheap restaurant	**en billig restaurang** *en bihl•eeg reh•stah•eu•rahng*
an expensive restaurant	**en dyr restaurang** *ehn dewr reh•stah•eu•rahng*

When it comes to eating out, there are many options, ranging from fast-food stands to five-star restaurants. If you are looking for a quick bite to eat, then a **gatukök** (fast-food stand) is an easy choice. If you are looking for more traditional cuisine, this can be found at a **värdshus** (roadside restaurant), **kafé** (cafe) or **restaurang** (restaurant).

Reservations & Preferences

I'd like to reserve a table...	**Jag skulle vilja boka ett bord...** *yahg skuh·ler vihl·ya boh·ka eht bohrd...*
for two	**för två** *furr tvoa*
for this evening	**till ikväll** *tihl ee·kvehl*
for tomorrow at...	**imorgon klockan...** *ee·mo·ron kloh·kan...*
A table for two, please.	**Kan jag få ett bord för två tack.** *kan yahg foa eht bohrd furr tvoa tak*
We have a reservation.	**Vi har bokat ett bord.** *vee hahr boa·kat eht bohrd*
My name is...	**Jag heter...** *yahg hee·tehr...*
Could we sit...?	**Får vi sitta...?** *foar vee siht·a...*
here/there	**här/där** *hair/dair*
outside	**ute** *eu·ter*
in a non-smoking area	**vid bord för icke-rökare** *veed bohrd furr ee·keh·rur·kah·rer*
by the window	**vid fönstret** *veed furns·treht*
in the shade	**i skuggan** *ee skuh·gan*
in the sun	**i solen** *ee sohl·ehn*

YOU MAY HEAR...

Har ni bokat? *hahr nee boh·kat*	Do you have a reservation?
Hur många blir ni? *heur moang·a bleer nee*	How many?
Rökare eller icke-rökare? *rur·ka·rer ehl·ehr ee·keh·rur·ka·rer*	Smoking or non-smoking?
Vill ni beställa? *vihl nee beh·steh·la*	Are you ready to order?
Vad vill ni beställa? *vahd vihl nee beh·steh·la*	What would you like?
Jag kan rekommendera... *yahg kan reh·koh·mehn·dee·ra...*	I recommend...
Smaklig måltid. *smahk·lihg moal·teed*	Enjoy your meal.

| Where are the restrooms [toilets]? | **Var finns toaletten?** *vahr fihns toa•ah•<u>leh</u>•tehn* |

How to Order

Excuse me!	**Ursäkta!** *<u>eur</u>•shehk•ta*
We're ready to order.	**Vi vill gärna beställa.** *vee vihl <u>yair</u>•na beh•<u>steh</u>•la*
May I see the wine list?	**Kan jag få se vinlistan?** *kan yahg foa see <u>veen</u>•lihs•tan*
I'd like…	**Jag skulle vilja ha…** *yahg <u>skuh</u>•ler <u>vihl</u>•ya hah…*
a bottle of…	**en flaska…** *ehn <u>flahs</u>•ka…*
a glass of…	**ett glas…** *eht glahs…*
a carafe of…	**en karaff…** *ehn kah•<u>raf</u>…*
The menu, please.	**En meny, tack.** *ehn meh•<u>neu</u> tak*
Do you have…?	**Har ni…?** *hahr nee…*
a menu in English	**en meny på engelska** *ehn meh•<u>neu</u> poa <u>ehng</u>•ehl•ska*
a fixed price menu	**en meny med fast pris** *ehn meh•<u>neu</u> meed fast prees*
a children's menu	**en barnmeny** *ehn <u>bahrn</u>•meh•neu*
What do you recommend?	**Vad rekommenderar ni?** *vahd reh•koh•mehn•<u>dee</u>•rar nee*
What's this?	**Vad är det här?** *vahd air dee hair*
What's in it?	**Vad är det i den?** *vahd air dee ee dehn*

Is it spicy?	**Är den kryddstark?** *air dehn <u>kreyd</u>•stark*
I'd like…	**Jag skulle vilja ha…** *yahg <u>skuh</u>•ler vihl•ya hah…*
More…, please.	**Lite mer…, tack.** *<u>lee</u>•teh meer…tak*
With/Without…	**Med/Utan…** *meed/<u>eu</u>•tan…*
I can't have…	**Jag kan inte äta mat som innehåller…** *yahg kan <u>ihn</u>•ter <u>air</u>•ta maht som <u>ih</u>•neh•hoal•lehr…*
rare	**blodig** *<u>bloa</u>•dihg*
medium	**medium** *<u>mee</u>•dee•uhm*
well done	**genomstekt** *<u>ye</u>•nom•steekt*
It's to go [take away].	**Jag ska ta den med mig.** *yahg skah tah dehn meed may*

For Drinks, see page 84.

YOU MAY SEE…

KUVERTAVGIFT	cover charge
FAST PRIS	fixed-price
MENY	menu
DAGENS MENY	menu of the day
DRICKS (INTE) INRÄKNAD	service (not) included
SPECIALITETER	specials

Cooking Methods

baked	**bakad** *<u>bah</u>•kad*
boiled	**kokt** *koakt*
braised	**bräserad** *braeh•<u>seeh</u>•rad*
breaded	**panerad** *pah•<u>neeh</u>•rad*
creamed	**rörd** *rurd*
diced	**i bitar** *ee <u>bee</u>•tar*
filleted	**filead** *fih•<u>leeh</u>•ad*

fried	**stekt** *steekt*
grilled	**grillad** *grihl·ad*
poached	**pocherad** *poa·sheeh·rad*
roasted	**ugnstekt** *eungn·steekt*
sautéed	**stekt** *steekt*
smoked	**rökt** *rurkt*
steamed	**ångkokt** *oang·koakt*
stewed	**stuvad** *steu·vad*
stuffed	**fylld** *fewld*

Dietary Requirements

I am…	**Jag är…** *yahg air…*
diabetic	**diabetiker** *dee·a·beh·tih·ker*
lactose intolerant	**laktosintolerant** *lak·toas·in·toh·leh·rant*
vegetarian	**vegetarian** *veh·geh·ta·ree·ahn*
vegan	**vegan** *veh·gahn*
I'm allergic to…	**Jag är allergisk mot…** *yahg air a·lehr·gihsk moat…*
I can't eat food	**Jag kan inte äta mat som innehåller…**
that contains…	*yahg kan ihn·ter air·ta maht som ihn·neh·hoa·lehr…*
dairy	**mejeriprodukter** *may·eh·ree·proh·duhk·tehr*
gluten	**gluten** *glue·tehn*
nut	**nöt** *nurt*
pork	**fläskkött** *flehsk·churt*
shellfish	**skaldjur** *skahl·yeur*
spicy food	**kryddad mat** *krew·dad maht*
wheat	**vete** *veeh·te*
Is it halal/kosher?	**Är det halal/kosher?** *air deht ha·lal/kosh·ehr*
Do you have…?	**Har ni…?** *hahr nee*
skimmed milk	**lättmjölk** *leht·myulk*
whole milk	**standardmjölk** *stahn·dardh·myulk*
soya milk	**sojamjölk** *soh·ya·myulk*

Dining with Children

Do you have a children's menu?	**Har ni en barnmeny?** *hahr nee ehn bahrn•meh•neu*
Can you bring a high chair, please?	**Kan jag få en barnstol, tack?** *kan yahg foa ehn bahrn•stoal tak*
Where can I feed/change the baby?	**Var kan jag mata/byta på babyn?** *vahr kan yahg mah•ta/bew•ta poa bai•been*
Can you warm this?	**Kan ni värma det här?** *kan nee vair•ma dee hair*

For Traveling with Children, see page 157.

How to Complain

How much longer will our food be?	**Hur länge till behöver vi vänta?** *heur lehng•er tihl beh•hur•ver vee vehn•ta*
We can't wait any longer.	**Vi kan inte vänta längre.** *vee kan ihn•ter vehn•ta lehng•rer*
We're leaving.	**Vi går nu.** *vee goar neu*
That's not what I ordered.	**Det här har jag inte beställt.** *dee hair hahr yahg ihn•ter beh•stehlt*
I asked for...	**Jag beställde...** *yahg beh•stehl•der...*
I can't eat this.	**Jag kan inte äta det här.** *yahg kan ihn•ter air•ta dee hair*
This is too...	**Det här är för...** *dee hair air furr...*
cold/hot	**kallt/varmt** *kalt/varmt*
salty/spicy	**salt/kryddat** *salt/krew•dat*
tough/bland	**segt/smaklöst** *sekt/smahk•lurst*
This isn't clean/fresh.	**Det här är inte rent/färskt.** *dee hair air ihn•ter reent/fairskt*

Paying

The check [bill], please.	**Kan jag få räkningen, tack.** *kan yahg foa rairk•nihng•ehn tak*

We'd like to pay separately.	**Vi vill betala var för sig.** *vee vihl beh·tah·la vahr furr say*	
It's all together.	**Allt tillsammans.** *alt tihl·saa·mans*	
Is service included?	**Är serveringsavgiften inräknad?** *air sehr·veeh·rihngs·afv·yihf·ten ihn·rairk·nad*	
What's this amount for?	**Vad står den här summan för?** *vahd stoar dehn hair suhm·an furr*	
I didn't have that. I had.	**Jag åt inte det. Jag åt…** *yahg oat ihn·ter dee yahg oat…*	
Can I pay by credit card?	**Kan jag betala med kreditkort?** *kan yahg beh·tah·la meed kreh·deet·koart*	
Can I have an itemized bill/ a receipt?	**Kan jag få en specificerad räkning/ett kvitto?** *kan yahg foa ehn speh·seh·fee·ee·rad rairk·nihng/ eht kvih·toh*	
That was a very good meal.	**Det var en mycket god måltid.** *dee vahr ehn mew·ker goad moal·teed*	
I've already paid	**Jag har redan betalat** *yahg hahr reh·dan beh·tah·lat*	

Meals & Cooking

Breakfast

apelsin *a·pehl·seen*	orange
bacon *bay·kohn*	bacon
bröd *brurd*	bread
filmjölk *feel·myurlk*	thick yogurt
frukostflingor *fruh·kohst·flihng·or*	(cold) cereal
fruktjuice *fruhkt·yoas*	fruit juice
grapefrukt *grape·fruhkt*	grapefruit
gröt *grurt*	(hot) cereal
havregryn *hafv·reh·greun*	oatmeal

Frukost (breakfast) is usually served from 7:00 to 10:00 a.m.
Hotels and guesthouses offer a large buffet selection of cheese,
cold meat, bread, eggs, cereals and **filmjölk** (thick yogurt). **Lunch**
(lunch) is served from as early as 11:00 a.m. Although many Swedes
have a warm meal at lunchtime, some opt for a sandwich or a salad.
This is the best time to try the **dagens rätt** (specialty of the day).
Middag (dinner) is normally eaten early, around 6:00 or 7:00 p.m.,
though many restaurants continue serving until late, especially at
the weekend. Many Swedes will also eat a meal later in the evening,
referred to as **kvällsmål;** this evening meal usually includes
sandwiches, yogurt or soup.

honung _hoa·neung_		honey
kaffe… _ka·fer…_		coffee…
med mjölk _meed myurlk_		with milk
med socker _meed soh·ker_		with sugar
med sötningsmedel		with artificial
meed surt·nihngs·mee·dehl		sweetener
utan koffein _eu·tan koh·feen_		decaf
kallskuret _kal·skeu·reht_		cold cuts [charcuterie]
kokt ägg _koakt ehg_		boiled egg
korv _kohrv_		sausage
marmelad _mar·meh·lahd_		marmalade
mjölk _myurlk_		milk
muffin _muh·fihn_		muffin
müsli _mews·lee_		granola [muesli]
omelett _ohm·eh·leht_		omelet
ost _oast_		cheese
rostat bröd _roahs·tat brurd_		toast

småbröd _smoa·brurd_	roll
smör _smur_	butter
stekt ägg _steekt ehg_	fried egg
sylt _sewlt_	jam
thé _tee_	tea
vatten _va·tehrn_	water
yoghurt _yoh·geurt_	yogurt
ägg _ehg_	egg
äggröra _ehg·rur·ra_	scrambled eggs
äpple _ehp·leh_	apple

Appetizers

färska räkor _fair·ska rair·kohr_	unshelled shrimp [prawns], served with toast, butter and mayonnaise
förrätt _furr·reht_	appetizer [starter]
gravlax _grafv·lax_	marinated salmon
löjrom _lurj·rohm_	bleak roe, served with chopped, raw onions and sour cream and eaten on toast
rökt lax _rurkt lax_	smoked salmon
sill _sihl_	marinated herring
sillbricka _sihl·brih·ka_	variety of marinated herring
S.O.S. (smör, ost och sill) _ehs oa ehs (smur oast ohk sil)_	a small plate of marinated herring, bread, butter and cheese
toast skagen _toast skah·gehn_	toast with chopped shrimp [prawns] in mayonnaise, topped with bleak roe
viltpastej _vihlt·pa·stay_	game pâté

Soup

buljong *beul·yong*	broth
fisksoppa *fihsk·sop·a*	fish soup
grönsakssoppa *grurn·sahks·sohp·a*	vegetable soup
kall soppa *kal sohp·a*	cold soup
kycklingsoppa *chewk·lihng·sohp·a*	chicken soup
kött och grönsakssoppa	meat and vegetable
churt·oa·grurn·sahk·sohp·a	soup
köttsoppa *churt·sohp·a*	a hearty soup of beef,
	vegetables and dumplings
löksoppa *lurk·sohp·a*	onion soup
nyponsoppa *new·pohn·sohp·a*	rose-hip soup
oxsvanssoppa *oax·svans·sohp·a*	oxtail soup
potatissoppa *poa·tah·tihs·sohp·a*	potato soup
rörd soppa *rurrd sohp·a*	cream soup
sparrissoppa *spa·rihs·sohp·a*	asparagus soup
spenatsoppa *speh·nat·sohp·a*	a rich soup made from
	spinach, potatoes, milk
	and cream
tomatsoppa *toa·maht·soh·pa*	tomato soup
ärtsoppa *airt·sohp·a*	green or yellow pea soup

Fish & Seafood

abborre *ah·bohr·er*	perch
ansjovis *an·shoa·vees*	anchovy
blåmussla *bloa·muhs·la*	blue mussel
braxen *brak·sehn*	sea bream
böckling *burk·lihng*	smoked Baltic herring
fisk *fihsk*	fish
forell *foa·rehl*	trout
färska räkor *fairs·ka rair·kohr*	unshelled shrimp [prawns]

gravlax *grafv·lax*	marinated salmon
gädda *yeh·da*	sea perch
halstrad fisk *hal·strahd fihsk*	grilled fish
halstrad forell med färskpotatis *hal·strad foa·rehl med fairsk·poa·tah·tihs*	grilled trout with new potatoes
havsabborre *hafs·a·boh·rer*	sea bass
hummer *huhm·ehr*	lobster
hälleflundra *heh·leh·fleun·dra*	halibut
inlagd sill *ihn·lagd sil*	marinated (pickled) herring
Janssons frestelse *yahn·sons frehs·tehl·ser*	casserole with potatoes and anchovies
kammussla *kam·muhs·la*	scallop
kolja *kohl·ya*	haddock
krabba *kra·ba*	crab
kräfta *krehf·ta*	crayfish
kummel *keu·mel*	hake
lax *lax*	salmon
löjrom *lury·rohm*	bleak roe with chopped, raw onions and sour cream; served on toast
makrill *mak·rihl*	mackerel
marulk *mahr·eulk*	monkfish
matjesill *ma·shcheh·sihl*	marinated herring
multe *muhl·ter*	mullet
mussla *muhs·la*	mussel
mört *murt*	roach (type of fish)
ostron *oas·tron*	oyster
piggvar *pihg·vahr*	turbot
rimmad lax med stuvad potatis *rihm·ahd lax meed steu·vad poa·tah·tihs*	lightly salted salmon with creamed potatoes and dill
rocka *roh·ka*	ray (type of fish)

räkor _rair_•kohr	shrimp [prawns]
röding _rur_•dihng	char
rödspätta _rurd_•speh•ta	plaice
rökt fisk _rur_kt fisk	smoked fish
rökt lax _rur_kt lax	smoked salmon
rökt ål _rur_kt oal	smoked eel
sardin sar•_deen_	sardine
sill sihl	herring
sillbricka _sihl_•brih•ka	variety of marinated herring
sillsallad _sihl_•sal•ad	beet and herring salad
sjötunga _sjur_•tuhng•a	sole
skaldjur _skahl_•yeur	shellfish
skaldjurssallad _skahl_•yeurs•sal•ad	shellfish salad
skarpsill _skarp_•sihl	herring
småsill _smoa_•sihl	herring
S.O.S. (smör, ost och sill) _ehs_ oa ehs (sm**ur** oast ohk sihl)	small plate of marinated herring, bread, butter and cheese
stekt fisk steekt fisk	fried fish
strömming _struhrm_•ihng	sprats (small Baltic herring) filleted and sandwiched in pairs with dill and butter in the middle
strömmingsflundra _strurm_•ihngs•fleun•dra	Baltic herring, filleted and sandwiched in pairs, fried, with dill and butter filling
stuvad abborre _steu_•vad _a_•boh•rer	perch poached with onion, parsley and lemon
tonfisk _toan_•fihsk	tuna
torsk tohrshk	cod
ugnsbakad fisk _eungns_•bah•kad fihsk	oven-baked fish

vitling _veet_·lihng	whiting
västkustsallad _vehst_·kuhst·_sal_·ad	west coast salad, with shrimp [prawns] and mussels
ål _oal_	eel
ångkokt fisk _oang_·koakt fisk	steamed fish

Meat & Poultry

anka _ang_·ka	duck
bacon _bay_·kon	bacon
biffkött _bihf_·churt	beef
biffstek _bihf_·steek	steak
bog _boag_	shoulder (cut of meat)
broiler _broy_·lehr	spring chicken
entrecote an·treh·_koat_	sirloin steak
falukorv _fah_·leu·kohrv	lightly spiced sausage
fasan fa·_sahn_	pheasant
filé fih·_leh_	filet mignon
fläsk _flehsk_	pork
fläskben _flehsk_·been	ham bone
fläskfilé _flehsk_·fih·_leh_	fillet of pork
fläskkarré _flehsk_·ka·_reh_	pork loin
fläskkorv _flehsk_·kohrv	spicy, boiled pork sausage
fläsklägg _flehsk_·lehg	knuckle of pork
fågel _foa_·gehl	poultry
får _foar_	mutton
get _yeet_	kid (goat)
grillad kyckling _grihl_·ahd _chewk_·lihng	grilled chicken
gås _goas_	goose
hamburgare _ham_·beur·ya·rer	hamburger
hare _hah_·rer	rabbit
hjort _yohrt_	deer

isterband _ihs·tehr·band_	sausage of pork, barley and beef
kalkon _kal·koan_	turkey
kallskuret _kal·skeu·reht_	cold cuts [charcuterie]
kalops _ka·lohps_	beef stew
kalvkött _kalv·churt_	veal
kalvsylta _kalv·sewl·ta_	cold veal in jelly
karré _ka·reh_	tenderloin
kokt skinka _koakt shihng·ka_	boiled ham
korv _kohrv_	sausage
kotlett _koht·lehtt_	cutlet
kyckling _chewk·lihng_	chicken
kycklingbröst _chewk·lihng·brurst_	chicken breast
kycklinglever _chewk·lihng·lee·vehr_	chicken liver
kåldomar med gräddsås och lingon _koal·dohl·mar meed grehd·soas ohk lihng·ohn_	chopped [minced] meat and rice stuffed in cabbage leaves
kött _churt_	meat
köttbulle _churt·buh·ler_	meatball
köttfärs _churt·fairs_	chopped [minced] beef
lamm _lamm_	lamb
lammgryta _lamm·grew·ta_	lamb stew
lever _lee·vehr_	liver
leverpastej _lee·vehr pa·stay_	liver pâté
lägg _lehg_	shank (top of leg)
lövbiff _lurv·bihf_	fried, thinly sliced beef, with onions
medaljong _meh·dal·yong_	small fillet of cut meat
njure _nyeu·rer_	kidney
nötkött _nurt·churt_	red meat
oxkött _oax·churt_	ox
oxrullad _oax·reu·lahd_	braised roll of beef

oxsvans _oax_·svans	oxtail
pannbiff _pan_·bihf	beef patty
prinskorv _prihns_·kohrv	small pork sausage
pärlhöns _pairl_·hurns	guinea fowl
ragu ra·_guh_	beef stew
rapphöna _rap_·_hurna_	partridge
ren reen	reindeer
renstek med svampsås _reen_·steek meed _svamp_·soas	roast reindeer with mushroom sauce
revbensspjäll _reev_·beens·spehl	spareribs
rostbiff _rohst_·bihf	roast beef
rumpstek _ruhmp_·steek	rump steak
rådjur _roa_·yeur	venison
rådjursstek _roa_·yeur·steek	roast of venison
rökt renstek rurkt _reen_·steek	smoked reindeer
rökt skinka rurkt _shihng_·ka	smoked ham
sadel _sah_·dehl	saddle (cut of meat)
salamikorv sa·lah·_mee_·kohrv	salami
schnitzel _shniht_·sehl	escallope
sillsallad _sihl_·sal·ad	beet and herring salad
sjömansbiff _shur_·mans·_bihf_	casserole of fried beef, onions and potatoes, braised in beer
skinka _shihng_·ka	ham
spädgris _spaird_·grees	an unweaned piglet
stekt kyckling steekt _chewk_·lihng	fried chicken (not breaded)
T-benstek _tee_·been·steek	T-bone steak
tunga _tuhng_·a	tongue (cow)
ugnsstekt kyckling _eungn_·steekt _chewk_·lihng	roast chicken
vaktel _vak_·tehl	quail
varmkorv _varm_·kohrv	hot dog
wienerschnitzel _vee_·nehr·shniht·sehl	breaded veal cutlet

If you've never heard of typical Swedish food, you may at least be familiar with the famous **smörgåsbord** — it is a buffet meal on a grand scale, presented on a large, beautifully decorated table. You start at one end of the table, usually the one with the cold seafood dishes, marinated herring, **Janssons frestelse** (literally, Jansson's temptation, a potato and anchovies casserole) and salad. Then you work your way through the cold meat, meatballs, sausage, omelets and vegetables. Finally, you end at the cheeseboard and desserts. You're welcome to start all over again; the price is set, and you can eat as much as you like. You will find that the Swedes tend to drink **akvavit** (aquavit) or beer with the feast, although an accompanying glass of wine is becoming more common for those who find **akvavit** too strong. At Christmas time, the **smörgåsbord** becomes a **julbord** (Christmas buffet), popular in homes and restaurants alike.

vildand *vihld·and*	wild duck
vilt *vihlt*	game
älg *ehly*	moose
älgfilé *ehly·fih·leh*	fillet of moose
älgstek *ehly·steek*	moose roast
älgstek med svampsås *ehly·steek meed svamp·soas*	roast moose with mushroom sauce

Vegetables & Staples

avokado *a·voh·kah·doa*	avocado
basilika *ba·sih·lee·ka*	basil
blandsallad *bland·sal·ad*	mixed salad
blomkål *bloam·koal*	cauliflower
bouquet garni *boh·keh gar·nee*	mixed herbs

böna... *bur·na...*	...bean
bond *boand*	broad
bryt *brewt*	kidney
grön *grurn*	green
vax *vax*	butter
broccoli *broh·koh·lee*	broccoli
brysselkål *brew·sehl·koal*	Brussel sprout
bröd *brurd*	bread
bönskott *burn·skoht*	bean sprout
champinjon *sham·pihn·yoan*	mushroom
chilipeppar *shee·lih·peh·par*	chili pepper
dragon *dra·goan*	tarragon
endiv *an·deev*	endive
fullkornsmjöl *fuhl·kohrns·myurl*	whole wheat flour
fänkål *fehn·koal*	fennel
färskpotatis *fairsk·poa·tah·this*	new potato
gräslök *grairs·lurk*	chive
grön paprika *grurn pah·pree·ka*	green pepper
grönsak *grurn·sahk*	vegetable
grönsallad *grurn·sal·ad*	lettuce
gurka *geur·ka*	cucumber
haricots verts *ar·ee·koh·vair*	green bean
honung *hoa·neung*	honey
ingefära *ih·ng·eh·fai·ra*	ginger
kanel *ka·neel*	cinnamon
kantarell *kan·ta·rehl*	chanterelle mushroom
kapris *ka·prees*	caper
kikärta *cheek·air·ta*	chickpea
kokt potatis *koakt poa·tah·tihs*	boiled potato
kronärtskocka *kroan·airts·koh·ka*	artichoke
kryddpeppar *krewd·peh·par*	allspice

kummin _keu·meen_	caraway
kål _koal_	cabbage
kålrot _koal·roht_	turnip
källkrasse _chehl·kra·ser_	watercress
körvel _chur·vehl_	chervil
lagerblad _lah·gehr·blahd_	bay leaf
lins _lihns_	lentil
lök _lurk_	onion
majs _mays_	sweet corn
mjöl _myurl_	flour
morot _moa·roht_	carrot
muskot _muhs·koht_	nutmeg
mynta _mewn·ta_	mint (herb)
nejlika _nay·lih·ka_	clove
nudel _neu·dehl_	noodle
olja och vinäger _oal·ya ohk vee·nai·gehr_	oil and vinegar
palsternacka _pal·stehr·na·ka_	parsnip
paprika _pah·prih·ka_	pepper (fresh)
pasta _pas·ta_	pasta
persilja _pair·shihl·ya_	parsley
potatis _poa·tah·tihs_	potato

potatissallad _poa_·_tah_·tihs·_sal_·ad	potato salad
pumpa _puhm_·pa	pumpkin
purjolök _peur_·yoh·_lurk_	leek
ris rees	rice
rosmarin roas·ma·_reen_	rosemary
rova _roa_·va	turnip
rädisa _raid_·dih·sa	radish
röd paprika rurd _pah_·pree·ka	sweet red pepper
rödbeta _rurd_·bee·ta	beet
rödkål _rurd_·_koal_	red cabbage
salladshuvud _sal_·ads·heu·vuhd	head of lettuce
saltgurka _salt_·geur·ka	salted, pickled gherkin
salvia sal·_vee_·a	sage
schalottenlök sha·_loh_·tehn·_lurk_	shallot [spring onion]
selleri seh·leh·_ree_	celery
sirap _seh_·rap	syrup
skogssvamp _skoags_·svamp	field mushroom
smör smurr	butter
sockerärta _soh_·kehr·air·ta	sugar snap pea [mangetout]
sparris _spar_·ihs	asparagus
spenat speh·_naht_	spinach
squash skoawsh	squash (vegetable)
svamp svamp	mushroom
sötpotatis _surt_·poa·_tah_·tihs	sweet potato
timjan tihm·_yan_	thyme
tomat toa·_maht_	tomato
tomater och lök toa·_mah_·ter ohk lurk	tomato and onion salad
vanilj va·_nihly_	vanilla
vattenkrasse _kra_·ser	watercress
vetemjöl _vee_·teh·_mjurl_	wheat flour (regular)
vild champinjon _vihl_·da sham·pihn·_yoan_	wild mushroom

vitkål _veet_•**koal**	white cabbage
vitlök _veet_•**lurk**	garlic
vårlök _voar_•**lurk**	shallot [spring onion]
zucchini seu•_kee_•nee	zucchini [courgette]
äggplanta _ehg_•plan•ta	eggplant [aubergine]
ärta _air_•ta	peas
ättiksgurka _eh_•tiks•geur•kah	pickled gherkin

Fruit

ananas _an_•a•nas	pineapple
apelsin a•pehl•_seen_	orange
aprikos a•prih•_koas_	apricot
banan ba•_nahn_	banana
bigarrå bih•ga•_roa_	sweet morello cherry
björnbär _byurn_•bair	blackberry
blå vindruva _bloa_ veen•dreu•va	black grape
blåbär _bloa_•bair	blueberry
citron see•_troan_	lemon
dadel _dahd_•ehl	date
enbär _een_•bair	juniper berry
fikon _fee_•kohn	fig
frukt fruhkt	fruit
grapefrukt _grape_•fruhkt	grapefruit
grön vindruva _grurn_ veen•dreu•va	green grape
hallon _hal_•ohn	raspberry
hasselnöt _ha_•sehl•nurt	hazelnut
hjortron _yoahr_•tron	cloudberry
jordgubbe _yoard_•guh•ber	strawberry
jordnöt _yoard_•nurt	peanut
katrinplommon ka•_treen_•ploa•mohn	prune
kiwifrukt _kee_•vee•fruhkt	kiwi

kokosnöt _koa·kos·nurt_	coconut
krusbär _kreus·bair_	gooseberry
körsbär _churs·bair_	cherry
lingon _lihng·ohn_	lingonberry
mandarin _man·da·reen_	tangerine/mandarin orange
mandel _man·dehl_	almond
(vatten)melon _(va·tehrn)meh·loan_	(water)melon
mullbär _muhl·bair_	mulberry
nektarin _nehk·ta·reen_	nectarine
oliv _o·leev_	olive
persika _pairsh·ih·ka_	peach
plommon _plohm·on_	plum
pomegranat äpple _pom·eh·gra·naht·ehp·leh_	pomegranate
päron _pai·rohn_	pear
rabarber _rah·bar·behr_	rhubarb
russin _ruh·sihn_	raisin
röd vinbär _rurd veen·bair_	red currant
smultron _smeul·trohn_	wild strawberry
sultana _suhl·tahn·a_	sultana raisin
svart vinbär _svart veen·bair_	black currant
valnöt _vahl·nurt_	walnut
vinbär _veen·bair_	currant
vindruva _veen·dreu·va_	grape
äpple _ehp·leh_	apple

Cheese

fårost _foar·oast_	ewe's milk cheese
getost _yeet·oast_	goat cheese
grevé _greh·vee_	a semi-hard cheese similar to gouda and emmentaler
herrgårdsost _hehr·goards·oast_	a semi-hard cheese with large holes and a nutty flavor

kryddost _krewd_•oast	a sharp, strong cheese with caraway seeds
mesost _mees_•oast	a soft, sweet, yellowish whey cheese
mjukost _myeuk_•oast	soft cheese
ost oast	cheese
ostbricka _oast_•brih•ka	cheese plate
prästost _prehst_•oast	hard cheese with a strong, rich flavor
svecia _sveh_•see•a	semi-hard cheeses
västerbotten _vehs_•tehr•_boh_•tehrn	a sharp, tangy, hard and very strong cheese from the north of Sweden
ädelost _air_•dehl•oast	a blue cheese with a sharp taste, similar to Roquefort

Dessert

efterrätt _ehf_•tehr•reht	dessert
friterad camembert med hjortronsylt _free_•_tee_•rad cam•ehm•_behrt_ meed _yoh_•tron•sewlt	deep-fried camembert with cloudberry jam
fruktsallad _frukht_•sal•ad	fruit salad
glass glas	ice cream
jordgubbar med grädde _yoard_•guhb•ar meed _greh_•deh	strawberries and cream
kaka _kah_•ka	cake
mandeltårta _man_•dehl•_toar_•ta	almond tart
marängsviss mah•_rehng_•svis	meringue with whipped cream and chocolate sauce
mjuk pepparkaka myeuk _peh_•par•kah•ka	soft ginger cake
ostkaka _oast_•kah•ka	traditional southern Sweden curd cake

tårta *toarta* — sponge-based fruit or cream cake

våffla (med sylt och grädde) *vohf·la meed sewlt ohk greh·der* — waffle (with jam and whipped cream)

äppelpaj *eh·pehl·pay* — apple tart

äppelkaka *eh·pehl·kah·ka* — apple cake

äppelring *ehp·ehl·rihng* — apple fritter

Sauces & Condiments

peppar *peh·par* — pepper

salt *salt* — salt

senap *see·nap* — mustard

socker *soh·kehr* — sugar

sötningsmedel *surt·nihngs·mee·dehl* — artificial sweetener

ketchup *keht·shuhp* — ketchup

At the Market

Where are the carts [trolleys]/baskets?	**Var finns shoppingvagnarna/shoppingkorgarna?** *vahr fihns shoh·pihng·vagn·nar·na/ shoh·pihng·kohr·yar·na*
Where is/are...?	**Var finns...?** *vahr fihns...*
I'd like some of this/that.	**Jag skulle vilja ha lite av det här/det där.** *yahg skuh·ler vihl·ya hah lee·teh afv dee hair/dee dair*

YOU MAY HEAR...

Kan jag hjälpa er? *kan yahg yehl·pa eer* — Can I help you?

Vad vill ni beställa? *vahd vihl nee beh·steh·la* — What would you like?

Något annat? *noa·goht an·nat* — Anything else?

Det kostar...kronor. *dee kos·tar...kroa·nohr* — That's...kronor.

YOU MAY SEE...

FÖRBRUKAS FÖRE...	best if used by...
KALORIER	calories
FETTFRI	fat free
MÅSTE FÖRVARAS I KYLSKÅP	keep refrigerated
KAN INNEHÅLLA SPÅR AV...	may contain traces of...
BÄST FÖRE...	sell by...
LÄMPLIGT FÖR VEGETARIANER	suitable for vegetarians

Can I taste it?	**Får jag smaka?** _foar yahg smah·ka_
I'd like...	**Jag skulle vilja ha...** _yahg skuh·ler vihl·ya hah..._
a kilo/half-kilo of...	**ett kilo/halvt kilo...** _eht chee·loh/halft chee·loh..._
a liter/half-liter of...	**en liter/halv liter...** _ehn lee·ter/halv lee·ter..._
a piece of...	**en bit av...** _ehn beet afv..._
a slice of...	**en skiva av...** _ehn shee·va afv..._
More/Less than that.	**Mer/Mindre än det där.** _meer/mihn·dreh ehn dee dair_
How much does it cost?	**Hur mycket kostar det?** _heur mew·ker kos·tar dee_
Where do I pay?	**Var kan jag betala?** _vahr kan yahg beh·tah·la_

Measurements in Europe are metric — and that applies to the weight of food too. If you tend to think in pounds and ounces, it's worth brushing up on what the equivalent is before you go shopping for fruit and veg in markets and supermarkets. Fivev hundred grams, or half a kilo, is a common quantity to order, and that converts to just over a pound (17.65 ounces, to be precise).

Although Sweden still has many small, specialty shops, they are slowly giving way to **köpcentrum** (shopping centers), especially in larger towns. You can still find markets that sell fresh fruit and vegetables as well as flowers and some handicrafts. **Julmarknaden** (the traditional Christmas market) in Stockholm is reminiscent of times gone by. Supermarkets can be found in most large towns, cities and suburbs. **Närbutiker** (corner shops), as well as **Pressbyrån** (newsstand chain) sell a good range of food. In Stockholm, **Östermalmshallen** and **Hötorgshallen** (market halls) sell fresh meat — including reindeer and moose — fish and poultry. Swedes enjoy a variety of fish and seafood, and one will find a good selection in most restaurants and supermarkets. If you visit Sweden in August, you will no doubt enjoy a **kräftkalas** (crayfish party). There is not much meat on a crayfish, but when helped down with a few glasses of **akvavit** (aquavit) and some salad and cheese, it makes for an unforgettable evening.

| Can I have a bag? | **Kan jag få en påse?** kan yahg foa ehn <u>poa</u>·seh |
| I'm being helped. | **Tack, jag har fått hjälp.** tak yahg hahr foat yehlp |

For Conversion Tables, see page 185.

In the Kitchen

bottle opener	**flasköppnare** <u>flask</u>·eup·na·rehr
bowl	**djup tallrik** yeup <u>tal</u>·rihk
can opener	**konservöppnare** kohn·<u>sehrv</u>·urp·nah·rer
corkscrew	**korkskruv** <u>kohrk</u>·skreuv
cup	**kopp** kohp
fork	**gaffel** <u>gahf</u>·ehl
frying pan	**stekpanna** <u>steek</u>·pan·na
glass	**glas** glahs

knife	**kniv** *kneev*
measuring cup/spoon	**mått/måttsked** *moat/moat·sheed*
napkin	**servett** *sehr·vehtt*
plate	**tallrik** *tal·rihk*
pot	**gryta** *grew·ta*
saucepan	**kastrull** *kas·truhl*
spatula	**steekspade** *steek·spah·der*
spoon	**sked** *sheed*

Drinks

ESSENTIAL

May I see the wine list/drink menu?	**Kan jag få se vinlistan/drinklistan?** *kan yahg foa see veen·lihs·tan/drihnk·lihs·tan*
What do you recommend?	**Vad rekommenderar ni?** *vahd reh·koh·mehn·dee·rar nee*
I'd like a bottle/glass of red/white wine.	**Jag skulle vilja ha en flaska/ett glas rött/vitt vin.** *yahg skuh·ler vihl·ya hah ehn flas·ka/eht glahs ruhrt/viht veen*
The house wine, please.	**Husets vin, tack.** *heu·sehts veen tak*
Another bottle/glass, please.	**En flaska/Ett glas till, tack.** *ehn flas·ka/eht glahs tihl tak*
I'd like a local beer.	**Jag skulle vilja ha en öl från trakten.** *yahg skuh·ler vihl·ya hah ehn url fron trak·tehn*
Let me buy you a drink.	**Får jag bjuda på en drink.** *foar yahg byeu·da poa ehn drihnk*
Cheers!	**Skål!** *skoal*
A coffee/tea, please.	**En kopp kaffe/te, tack.** *ehn kohp ka·fer/tee tak*

Black.	**Svart.** *Svart*	
With…	**Med…** *meed…*	
milk	**mjölk** *myuhlk*	
sugar	**socker** *soh·kehr*	
artificial sweetener	**sötningsmedel** *surt·nihngs·mee·dehl*	
decaf	**utan koffein** *eu·tan koh·feen*	
…, please.	**…, tack.** *…tak*	
Juice	**Juice** *yoas*	
Soda	**sodavatten** *soa·da·va·tehrn*	
Sparkling water	**Vatten med kolsyra** *va·tehrn meed koal·sew·ra*	
Still water	**Vatten utan kolsyra** *va·tehrn eu·tan koal·sew·ra*	
Is the tap water safe to drink?	**Kan man dricka kranvattnet?** *kan man drih·ka krahn·vat·neht*	

Non-alcoholic Drinks

alkoholfri dryck *al·ko·hoal·free drewk*	non-alcoholic drink
ananasjuice *an·a·nas·yoas*	pineapple juice
apelsinjuice *a·pehl·seen·yoas*	orange juice
cola *koa·la*	cola
fruktjuice *fruhkt·yoas*	fruit juice
juice *yoas*	juice
kaffe *ka·fer*	coffee
läsk *lehsk*	soft drink
milkshake *milk·shake*	milk shake
mineralvatten *mihn·eh·rahl·va·tehrn*	mineral water
mjölk *myurlk*	milk
saft *saft*	squash (fruit cordial)
sockerdricka *soh·kehr·drih·ka*	lemonade
sodavatten *soa·da·va·tehrn*	soda water

YOU MAY HEAR...

Får jag bjuda på en drink? *foar yahg* *bjeu-da pao ehn drink*

Can I buy you a drink?

Med mjölk/socker? *meed myurlk/soh-ker*

With milk/sugar?

Vatten med/utan kolsyra? *va-tehrn meed/* *eu-tan koal-sew-ra*

Sparkling/Still water?

thé med mjölk/citron *tee meed myurlk/* *see-troan*

tea with milk/lemon

tomatjuice *toa-maht-yoas*

tomato juice

tonic *toh-nihk*

tonic water

varmchoklad *varm shoa-klahd*

hot chocolate

vatten med/utan kolsyra *va-tehrn meed/* *eu-tan koal-sew-ra*

sparkling/still water

For afternoon tea (usually enjoyed with lemon) or coffee you can do no better than the typical Swedish **konditori** (patisserie or coffee shop). Help yourself to as many cups as you like while indulging in a slice of **prinsesstårta** (sponge cake with cream and custard, covered with green marzipan), **mazarin** (almond tart, topped with icing) or a **wienerbröd** (Danish pastry). Try **saffransbullar** (saffron buns) and **pepparkakor** (ginger cookies) at Christmas. Most **konditori** are self-service, but some of the more elegant ones and those in hotels provide full service. Coffee is definitely the national drink, and it is always freshly brewed. It is commonly drunk black, but ask for **mjölk** (milk) or **grädde** (cream) if you like it that way.

Aperitifs, Cocktails & Liqueurs

akvavit *a·kva·veet*	aquavit, the famous Swedish grain- or potato-based spirit
cognac *kohn·yak*	brandy
gin *jihn*	gin
glögg *glurg*	mulled wine with port and spices, served hot
herrgårdsakvavit *hair·goards·a·kva·veet*	aquavit, flavored with caraway seeds and whisky
likör *lih·kurr*	liqueur
portvin *port·veen*	port
punsch *peunsh*	sweet liqueur
rom *rohm*	rum
sherry *sheh·ree*	sherry
skåne *skoa·ner*	aquavit, flavored with aniseed and caraway seeds
sprit *spreet*	spirits
vermouth *vehr·meutt*	vermouth
vodka... *vod·ka...*	vodka...
med is *meed ees*	on the rocks [with ice]
med tonic *meed toh·nihk*	with tonic water

med vatten *meed va·tehrn*	with water
whisky *vihs·kee*	whisky

Beer

burköl *buhrk·url*	canned beer
fatöl *faht·url*	draft [draught]
lättöl *leht·url*	light beer
öl på flaska *url poa fla·ska*	bottled beer local/imported
utan alkohol *uh·tan al·koh·hohl*	non-alcoholic

Beer is probably the most popular alcoholic drink in Sweden, and there are many good Swedish breweries. Beer with an alcohol content above 3%, called **starköl**, can only be bought in **Systembolaget** (state liquor store); **lättöl** and **folköl**, which are below 3% alcohol content, can be bought in grocery stores and supermarkets. You will find many well known international beers, but the most common are Carlsberg, Heineken and Swedish brews such as Pripps and Falcon.

Wine

dessertvin *deh·sair·veen*	dessert wine
husets vin *heu·sehts veen*	house wine
mousserande *moa·see·ran·der*	sparkling
rosé *roh·seh*	blush [rosé]
rött *ruhrt*	red
sött *suhrt*	sweet
torrt *tohrt*	dry
vitt *viht*	white
champagne *shahm·pany*	champagne

On the Menu

abborre *ah•bohr•er*   perch
akvavit *a•kva•<u>veet</u>*   aquavit, the famous Swedish
                                          grain- or potato-based spirit
alkoholfri dryck *al•ko•<u>hoal</u>•free drewk*   non-alcoholic drink
ananas *<u>an</u>•a•nas*   pineapple
ananasjuice *<u>an</u>•a•nas•yoas*   pineapple juice
anka *<u>ang</u>•ka*   duck
ansjovis *an•<u>shoa</u>•vees*   anchovy
apelsin *a•pehl•<u>seen</u>*   orange
apelsinjuice *a•pehl•<u>seen</u>•yoas*   orange juice
aprikos *a•prih•<u>koas</u>*   apricot
avokado *a•voh•<u>kah</u>•doa*   avocado
bacon *<u>bay</u>•kon*   bacon
bakelse *<u>bah</u>•kehl•sehr*   piece of cake
bakverk *<u>bahk</u>•verk*   pastry
banan *ba•<u>nahn</u>*   banana
basilika *ba•sih•<u>lee</u>•ka*   basil
biffkött *<u>bihf</u>•churt*   beef
biffstek *<u>bif</u>•steek*   steak

bigarrå _bih·ga·roa_	sweet morello cherry
bit _beet_	slice
björnbär _byurn·bair_	blackberry
blandade _blan·da·der_	assorted
blandade grönsaker _blan·da·der grurn·sah·kehr_	mixed vegetables
blandade kryddor _blan·da·der krew·dohr_	mixed herbs
blandade nötter _blan·da·der nur·tehr_	assorted nuts
blandsallad _bland·sal·ad_	mixed salad
blodig _bloa·dihg_	rare
blomkål _bloam·koal_	cauliflower
blå vindruva _bloa veen·dreu·va_	black grape
blåbär _bloa·bair_	blueberry
blåbärssylt _bloa·bairs·sewlt_	blueberry jam
blåmussla _bloa·muhs·la_	blue mussel
bog _boag_	shoulder (cut of meat)
bondböna _boand·bur·nohr_	broad bean
bordsvin _boards·veen_	table wine
bouquet garni _boh·keh gar·nee_	mixed herbs
braxen _brak·sehn_	sea bream
broccoli _broh·loh·lee_	broccoli

broiler _broy_·lehr	spring chicken
brylépudding brew·_lee_·peu·dihng	crème brulee
brysselkål _brew_·sehl·_koal_	brussel sprout
brytböna _brewt_·bur·na	kidney bean
brännvin _brehn_·veen	aquavit, grain or potato based spirit
bröd _brurd_	bread
brödsmulor _brurd_·smeu·lohr	bread crumbs
bröst brurst	breast
buljong buhl·_yong_	broth
bulle _buh_·ler	bun
burköl _buhrk_·url	canned beer
bål boal	punch
böckling _burk_·lihng	smoked herring
böna _bur_·na	bean [pulses]
bönskott _burn_·skoht	bean sprout
champinjon sham·pihn·_yoan_	mushroom
chilipeppar _shee_·lih·_peh_·par	chili pepper
chips shihps	potato chips [crisps]
choklad shoa·_klahd_	chocolate
citron see·_troan_	lemon
citronjuice see·_troan_·yoas	lemon juice
cognac _kohn_·yak	brandy
cola _koa_·la	cola
dadel _dahd_·ehl	date
dagens meny _dah_·gehns meh·_neu_	menu of the day
dagens rätt _dah_·gehns rairtt	speciality of the day
dessertvin deh·_sair_·veen	dessert wine
dillsås _dihl_·soas	dill sauce
dragon dra·_goan_	tarragon
dryck med alkohol drewk meed _al_·ko·hoal	alcoholic drink

efterrätt _ehf·tehr·rairt_	dessert
en halv flaska _ehn halv fla·ska_	half bottle
enbär _een·bair_	juniper berry
endiv _an·deev_	endive
entrecote _an·treh·koa_	sirloin steak
falukorv _fah·leu·kohrv_	lightly spiced sausage
fasan _fa·sahn_	pheasant
fatöl _faht·url_	draft [draught] beer
fikon _fee·kohn_	fig
filé _fih·leh_	filet mignon
filmjölk _feel·mjurlk_	thick yogurt
fisk _fihsk_	fish
fisk och skaldjur _fihsk·ohk·skahl·yeur_	fish and seafood
fisksoppa _fihsk·sop·a_	fish soup
fläsk _flehsk_	pork
fläskben _flehsk·been_	ham bone
fläskfilé _flehsk·fih·leh_	fillet of pork
fläskkarré _flehsk·ka·reh_	pork loin
fläskkorv _flehsk·kohrv_	spicy, boiled pork sausage
fläsklägg _flehsk·lehg_	knuckle of pork
fläskpannkaka	thick pancake filled
flehsk·pan·kah·ka	with bacon
forell _foa·rehl_	trout
franskbröd _fransk·brurd_	French bread
friterad camembert med hjortronsylt	deep-fried Camembert
free·tee·rad cam·ehm·behrt meed yoh·tron·sewlt	with cloudberry jam
frukost _fruh·kohst_	breakfast
frukostflingor _fruhkost·flihng·ohr_	(cold) cereal
frukt _fruhkt_	fruit
fruktjuice _fruhkt·yoas_	fruit juice
fruktsallad _fruhkt·sal·ad_	fruit salad

fullkornsmjöl _fuhl_·kohrns·my**url**	whole wheat flour
fylld (med) fewld (meed)	stuffed (with)
fylld oliv _fewld_ o·_leev_	stuffed olive
fylligt _few_·liht	full-bodied (wine)
fågel _foa_·gehl	poultry
får foar	mutton
fårost _foar_·oast	ewe's milk cheese
fänkål _fehn_·k_oal_	fennel
färsk (frukt) fehrsk (fruhkt)	fresh (fruit)
färsk fikon fairsk _fee_·kohn	fresh fig
färska räkor _fairs_·ka _rair_·kohr	unshelled shrimp [prawns]
färskpotatis _fairsk_·poa·_tah_·tihs	new potato
förlorat ägg furr·_loa_·rat ehg	poached egg
förrätt _furr_·rairt	appetizer [starter]
garnering gar·_nee_·rihng	garnish
gelé sheh·_leh_	jelly
get yeet	kid (goat)
getost _yeet_·oast	goat cheese
gin jihn	gin
glass glas	ice cream
glutenfritt _glue_·tehn·friht	gluten free

glögg *glurg* — mulled wine with port and spices, served hot

grapefrukt *grahp*-fruhkt — grapefruit

gratinerad *gra*-tih-*nee*-rad — au gratin

gratäng *gra*-tehng — casserole

gravlax *grafv*-lax — marinated salmon

grevé *greh*-*veh* — semi-hard cheese

grillad kyckling *grihl*-ahd *chewk*-lihng — grilled chicken

grillspett *grihl*-speht — skewer

gryta *grew*-ta — pot roast, stew or casserole

grädde *greh*-der — cream

gräddfil *grehd*-feel — sour cream

gräslök *grairs*-*lurk* — chive

grön böna *grur*-na *bur*-na — green bean

grön paprika grurn *pah*-pree-ka — green pepper

grön vindruva *grur*n veen-dr**eu**-va — green grape

grönsak *grurn*-sahk — vegetable

grönsakssoppa *grurn*-sahks-*sohp*-a — vegetable soup

grönsallad *grurn*-sal-ad — green salad

gröt *grurt* — (hot) cereal

gurka *geur*-ka — cucumber

gås *goas* — goose

gädda *yeh*-da — sea perch

hallon *hal*-ohn — raspberry

halstrad fisk *hal*-strahd fihsk — grilled fish

halstrad forell med färskpotatis *hal*-strad foa-*rehl* med *fairsk*-poa-*tah*-this — grilled trout with new potatoes

hamburgare *ham*-beur-ya-rer — hamburger

hare *hah*-rer — rabbit

haricots verts ar-ee-koh-*vair* — string beans

hasselbackspotatis _ha_·sehl·baks·poa·_tah_·tihs	oven-baked potato, coated in bread crumbs
hasselnöt _ha_·sehl·nurt	hazelnut
havre _hafv_·rer	oats
havregryn _hafv_·reh·greun	oatmeal
havsabborre _hafs_·a·boh·rer	sea bass
hemlagad _hehm_·lah·gad	homemade
herrgårdsakvavit _hair_·**go**ards·a·kva·_veet_	aquavit flavored with caraway seeds and whisky
herrgårdsost _hehr_·goards·oast	semi-hard cheese with a nutty flavor
hett heht	hot (temperature)
hjort yohrt	deer
hjortron _yoahr_·tron	cloudberry
hjortron sylt _yoar_·trohn·sewlt	cloudberry jam
honung hoa·neung	honey
hovmästarsås _hoav_·mehs·tar·**so**as	dill sauce
hummer _huhm_·ehr	lobster
husets specialitet _heu_·sehts speh·sih·al·ee·_teet_	specialty of the house
husets vin _heu_·sehts veen	house wine
huvudrätt _heu_·vuhd·rait	main course

hårdkokt ägg _hoard·kohkt ehg_	hard-boiled egg
hårt bröd _hoart brurd_	crispbread
hälleflundra _heh·leh·fleun·dra_	halibut
ingefära _ih·ng·eh·fai·ra_	ginger
inlagd i ättika (vinäger) _ihn·lahgd ee eh·tih·ka_	marinated in vinegar
inlagd sill _ihn·lahgd sil_	marinated (pickled) herring
is _ees_	ice
isterband _ihs·tehr·band_	sausage of pork, barley and beef
Janssons frestelse _yahn·sons frehs·tehl·ser_	casserole with potatoes and anchovies
jordgubbar med grädde _yoard·guhb·ar meed greh·deh_	strawberries and cream
jordgubbe _yoard·guh·ber_	strawberry
jordnöt _yoard·nurt_	peanut
juice _yoas_	juice
julbord _yeul·board_	buffet of hot and cold Swedish specialties served at Christmas time
kaffe _ka·fer_	coffee

kaka *kah·ka*	cake
kalkon *kal·koan*	turkey
kall soppa *kal sohp·a*	cold soup
kallskuret *kal·skeu·reht*	cold cuts
kalops *ka·lohps*	beef stew
kalvbräss *kalv·brehs*	sweetbread
kalvkött *kalv·churt*	veal
kalvsylta *kalv·sewl·ta*	cold veal in jelly
kammussla *kam·muhs·la*	scallop
kanderad frukt *kan·deeh·rahd fruhkt*	candied fruit
kanel *ka·neel*	cinnamon
kantarell *kan·ta·rehl*	chanterelle mushroom
kapris *ka·prees*	caper
karaff *ka·raff*	carafe
karameller *ka·ra·mehl·ehr*	candy [sweets]
karré *ka·reh*	tenderloin
katrinplommon *ka·treen·ploa·mohn*	prune
kex *kehx*	cookie [biscuit]
kikärta *cheek·air·ta*	chickpea
kiwifrukt *kee·vee·fruhkt*	kiwi
klimp *klihmp*	dumpling
kokosnöt *koa·kos·nurt*	coconut
kokt katrinplommon *koakt ka·treen·ploa·mohn*	stewed prune
kokt potatis *koakt poa·tah·tihs*	boiled potato
kokt skinka *koakt shihng·ka*	boiled ham
kokt ägg *koakt ehg*	boiled egg
kolja *kohl·ya*	haddock
kolsyrad *koal·sew·rad*	carbonated
kompott *kom·poht*	stewed fruit
konserverad frukt *kon·ser·vee·rad fruhkt*	canned fruit

korv *kohrv*	sausage
kotlett *koht·lehtt*	cutlet
krabba *kra·ba*	crab
kronärtskocka *kroan·airts·koh·ka*	artichoke
kroppkaka *kropp·kah·ka*	potato dumpling, filled with bacon and onions
krusbär *kreus·bair*	gooseberry
krydda *krew·da*	spice
kryddad *krew·dad*	spicy
kryddad pepparsås *krew·dahd peh·par·soas*	hot pepper sauce
kryddost *krewd·oast*	sharp, strong cheese with caraway seeds
kryddpeppar *krewd·peh·par*	allspice
kryddstarkt *krewd·starkt*	spicy
kräfta *krehf·ta*	crayfish
kummel *keu·mel*	hake
kummin *keu·meen*	caraway
kvark *kvark*	fresh curd cheese
kyckling *chewk·lihng*	chicken
kycklingbröst *chewk·lihng·brurst*	chicken breast
kycklinglever *chewk·lihng·lee·vehr*	chicken liver
kycklingsoppa *chewk·lihng·sohp·a*	chicken soup
kyld dryck *chewl drewk*	cold drink
kylt *chewlt*	chilled (wine, etc.)
kål *koal*	cabbage
kåldolmar *koal·dohl·mar*	cabbage leaves stuffed with chopped [minced] meat and rice
kålrot *koal·roht*	turnip
källkrasse *chehl·kra·se*	watercress
körsbär *churs·bair*	cherry

körvel _chur·vehl_	chervil
kött _churt_	meat
kött och grönsakssoppa _churt·oa·grurn·sahk·sohp·a_	meat and vegetable soup
köttbulle _churt·buh·ler_	meatball
köttfärs _churt·fairs_	chopped [minced] beef
köttsoppa _churt·sohp·a_	beef and vegetable soup with dumplings
köttsås _churt·soas_	meat sauce
lagerblad _lah·gehr·blahd_	bay leaf
lageröl _lah·ger·url_	lager
lamm _lamm_	lamb
lammgryta _lamm·grew·ta_	lamb stew
landgång _land·goang_	long open-faced sandwich
lax _lax_	salmon
lever _lee·vehr_	liver
leverpastej _lee·vehr pa·stay_	liver pâté
lingon _lihng·ohn_	lingonberry
lingonsylt _lihng·ohn·sewlt_	lingonberry jam
lins _lihns_	lentil
likör _lih·kurr_	liqueur

lägg *lehg*	shank (top of leg)
läsk *lehsk*	soft drink
lättöl *leht·ur*	light beer
löjrom *lury·rohm*	bleak roe with chopped, raw onions and sour cream; served on toast
lök *lurk*	onion
löksoppa *lurk·sohp·a*	onion soup
lövbiff *lurv·bihf*	fried, thinly sliced beef, with onions
majonnäs *may·oha·nairs*	mayonnaise
majs *mays*	sweet corn
makrill *mahk·rihl*	mackerel
mandarin *man·da·reen*	tangerine/mandarin orange
mandel *man·dehl*	almond
mandeltårta *man·dehl·toar·ta*	almond tart
marmelad *mahr·meh·lahd*	marmalade
marsipan *mahr·sih·pahn*	marzipan
marulk *mahr·eulk*	monkfish
maräng *mah·rehng*	meringue
marängsviss *mah·rehng·svihs*	meringue served with cream and chocolate sauce

matjesill *ma·shcheh·sihl*	marinated herring
med citron *meed see·troan*	with lemon
med florsocker *meed floar·soh·ker*	with icing
med grädde *meed greh·der*	with cream
med is *meed ees*	with ice
med kolsyra *meed koal·sew·ra*	carbonated (drink)
med mjölk *meed myurlk*	with milk
med socker *meed soh·kehr*	with sugar
med tonic *meed toh·nihk*	with tonic water
med vatten *meed va·tehrn*	with water
med vitlök *meed veet·lurk*	with garlic
medaljong *meh·dal·yong*	small fillet of cut meat
medium *meh·dee·yuhm*	medium
mellanmål *meh·lan·moal*	snack
(vatten)melon *(va·tehrn)meh·loan*	(water)melon
meny *meh·neu*	menu
mesost *mees·oast*	soft, sweet whey cheese
middag *mih·dahg*	dinner
milkshake *milk·shake*	milk shake
mineralvatten *mih·neh·rahl·va·tehrn*	mineral water
mjuk pepparkaka *myeuk peh·par·kah·ka*	soft ginger cake
mjukost *myeuk·oast*	soft cheese
mjöl *myurl*	flour
mjölk *myurlk*	milk
mogen *moa·gehn*	ripe
morot *moa·roht*	carrot
mousserande *moa·see·ran·der*	sparkling (wine)
muffin *muh·fihn*	muffin
mullbär *muhl·bair*	mulberry
multe *muhl·ter*	mullet
munk *muhnk*	donut

muskot _muhs_·koht — nutmeg
müsli _mews_·lee — granola [muesli]
mussla _muhs_·la — mussel
mustigt _muhs_·tihkt — full-bodied (wine)
mycket kryddad _mew_·keht _krew_·dad — highly seasoned
mycket torrt _mew_·keht tohrt — very dry (wine, etc.)
mynta _mewn_·ta — mint (herb)
mäktig _mehk_·tihg — rich (sauce)
mördegstårta _muhr_·deegs·_toar_·ta — tart (sweet or savory)
mört murtt — roach (type of fish)
nejlika _nay_·lih·ka — clove
nektarin nehk·ta·_reen_ — nectarine
njure _nyeu_·rer — kidney
nudel _neu_·dehl — noodle
nyponsoppa _new_·pohn·sohp·a — rose-hip soup
nötkött _nurt_·churt — red meat
odlade champinjon _oad_·lah·der sham·peen·_yoan_ — cultivated mushroom
ojäst bröd oa·_yai_rst brurd — unleavened bread
oliv o·_leev_ — olive
olja och vinäger _oal_·ya ohk vee·_nai_·gehr — oil and vinegar
omelett om·eh·_leht_ — omelet
ost oast — cheese
ostbricka _oast_·brih·ka — cheese plate
ostkaka _oast_·kah·ka — curd cake served with jam
ostkex _oast_·kehx — cheese cracker
ostron _oa_·strohn — oyster
oxkött _oax_·churt — ox
oxrullad _oax_·reu·_lahd_ — braised roll of beef
oxsvans _oax_·svans — oxtail
oxsvanssoppa _oax_·svans·_sohp_·a — oxtail soup

paj *pay* — pie

palsternacka *pal·stehr·na·ka* — parsnip

pannbiff *pan·bihf* — beef patty

pannkaka *pan·kah·ka* — pancake

paprika *pah·prih·ka* — pepper (fresh)

pasta *pas·ta* — pasta

pastarätt *pas·ta·rairt* — pasta dish

pastej *pa·stay* — pâté

peppar *peh·par* — pepper (condiment)

pepparkaka *peh·par·kah·ka* — ginger cookie

pepparrotssås *peh·pa·roat·soas* — horseradish sauce

persika *pair·shih·ka* — peach

persilja *pair·shihl·ya* — parsley

piggvar *pihg·vahr* — turbot

pitabröd *pee·ta·brurd* — pita bread

plommon *ploa·mohn* — plum

plättar *pleh·tar* — small pancakes served with jam and whipped cream

pomegranat äpple *pom·eh·gra·naht·ehp·leh* — pomegranate

pommes frites *pohm·friht* — French fries

portion *pohrt·shoan* — portion

portvin _pohrt_·veen	port
potatis poa·_tah_·tihs	potato
potatismos poa·_tah_·tihs·moas	mashed potatoes
potatissoppa poa·**_tah_**·tihs·_sohp_·a	potato soup
prinsesstårta prihn·_sehs_·**toar**·ta	sponge cake with (vanilla) custard, whipped cream and jam, covered in light green marzipan
prinskorv _prihns_·kohrv	small pork sausage
prästost _prehst_·oast	hard cheese with a strong, rich flavor
pumpa _puhm_·pa	pumpkin
punsch peunsh	sweet liqueur
purjolök _peur_·yoh·**lurk**	leek
pytt i panna _pewt_·ee·pa·na	chunks of fried meat, onion and potatoes
på beställning poa beh·_stehl_·nihng	made on request
pärlande _pair_·lan·der	sparkling
pärlhöns _pairl_·hurns	guinea fowl
päron _pai_·rohn	pear
rabarber rah·_bar_·behr	rhubarb

ragu _ra·gue_ — beef stew

rapphöna _rap·hurna_ — partridge

ren _reen_ — reindeer

renat _ree·nat_ — flavorless, clear spirit (aquavit)

renstek _reen·steek_ — roast reindeer

revbensspjäll _reev·beens·spehl_ — spareribs

riktigt blodig _rihk·tihgt bloa·dihg_ — very rare

rimmad lax _rih·mad lax_ — lightly salted salmon

ris _rees_ — rice

rocka _roh·ka_ — ray (type of fish)

rom _rohm_ — rum

rosé _roh·seh_ — blush (wine)

rosmarin _roas·ma·reen_ — rosemary

rostat bröd _rohs·tat brurd_ — toast

rostbiff _rohst·bihf_ — roast beef

rova _roa·va_ — turnip

rumpstek _ruhmp·steek_ — rump steak

russin _ruh·sihn_ — raisin

rå _roa_ — raw

rådjur _roa·yeur_ — venison

rådjursstek _roa·yeur·steek_ — roast of venison

rågbröd _roag·brurd_ — rye bread

rädisa _raid·dih·sa_ — radish

räkor _rair·kohr_ — shrimp [prawns]

rätt _reht_ — dish

röd paprika _rurd pah·pree·ka_ — sweet red pepper

röd vinbär _rurd veen·bair_ — red currant

rödbeta _rurd·bee·ta_ — beet

röding _rur·dihng_ — char

rödkål _rurd·koal_ — red cabbage

rödspätta _rurd_·speh·ta	plaice
rökt fisk _rurkt_ fisk	smoked fish
rökt lax _rurkt_ lax	smoked salmon
rökt renstek _rurkt_ _reen_·steek	smoked reindeer
rökt skinka _rurkt_ _shihng_·ka	smoked ham
rökt ål _rurkt_ oal	smoked eel
rörd soppa rurrd _sohp_·a	cream soup
rött rurt	red (wine)
sadel _sah_·dehl	saddle (cut of meat)
saffransbullar _sa_·frans·buh·lar	Christmas saffron buns
saft saft	squash (fruit cordial)
salamikorv sa·lah·_mee_·kohrv	salami
sallad _sal_·ad	salad
salladshuvud _sal_·ads·heu·vuhd	head of lettuce
salt salt	salt
saltade jordnötter _sal_·ta·der _yoard_·nur·ter	salted peanuts
saltgurka _salt_·geur·ka	salted, pickled gherkin
salvia sal·_vee_·a	sage
sardin sar·_deen_	sardine
schalottenlök sha·loh·_tehn_·lurk	shallot
schnitzel _shniht_·sehl	escallope
selleri seh·leh·_ree_	celery
senap _see_·nap	mustard
sherry sheh·_ree_	sherry
sill sihl	herring
sillbricka _sihl_·brih·ka	variety of marinated herring
sillsallad _sihl_·sal·ad	beet and herring salad
sirap _seh_·rap	syrup
sjömansbiff _shur_·mans·bihf	casserole of fried beef, onions and potatoes, braised in beer
sjötunga _sjur_·teung·a	sole

skaldjur _skahl_•ye*ur*	shellfish
skaldjurssallad _skahl_•ye*ur*s•sal•ad	shellfish salad
skarpsill _skarp_•sihl	herring
skinka _skihng_•ka	ham
skogssvamp _skoags_•svamp	field mushroom
sky she*wy*	gravy
skåne _skoa_•ner	type of aquavit flavored with aniseed and caraway
smultron _smeul_•trohn	wild strawberry
småbröd _smoa_•bru*rd*	roll
småkaka _smoa_•kah•ka	cookie [biscuit]
smårätt _smoa_•rairt	snack
småsill _smoa_•sihl	herring
smör smu*r*	butter
smördeg _smur_•deeg	pastry
smörgås _smur_•goas	Swedish open-faced sandwich
snigel _sneeg_•ehl	snail
socker _soh_•kehr	sugar
sockerdricka _soh_•kehr•drih•ka	lemonade
sockerkaka _soh_•kehr•kah•ka	sponge cake

sockerärta _soh·kehr·air·ta_	sugar snap pea [mangetout]
sodavatten _soa·da·va·tehrn_	soda water
soppa _sohp·a_	soup
S.O.S. (smör, ost och sill) _ehs oa ehs_ _(smur oast ohk sihl)_	small plate of marinated herring, read, butter and cheese
sparris _spar·ihs_	asparagus
sparrissoppa _spa·rihs·sohp·a_	asparagus soup
specialitet för landsdelen _speh·sih·ahl·ih·teet furr lands·deel·ehn_	local specialty
spenat _speh·naht_	spinach
spenatsoppa _speh·naht·sohp·a_	spinach soup
sprit _spreet_	spirits
spädgris _spaird·grees_	unweaned piglet
squash _skoawsh_	squash (vegetable)
stark _stark_	strong (flavor)
starkt kryddad _starkt krew·dad_	hot (spicy)
stek _steek_	roast
stekt fisk _steekt fisk_	fried fish
stekt kyckling _steekt chewk·lihng_	fried chicken (not breaded)
stekt potatis _steekt poa·tah·tihs_	sautéed potato
stekt ägg _steekt ehg_	fried egg
strömming _strurm·ihng_	sprats (small Baltic herring)
strömmingsflundra _strurm·ihngs·fleun·dra_	Baltic herring, filleted and sandwiched in pairs, fried, with dill and butter filling
stuvad abborre _steu·vad a·bohr·er_	perch poached with onion, parsley and lemon
sufflé _suh·fleh_	soufflé
sultana _suhl·tahn·a_	sultana raisin
sur _seur_	sour

svamp *svamp*	mushroom
svart vinbär *svart veen·bair*	black currant
svecia *sveh·see·a*	semi-hard cheese
svensk punsch *sven·sk peunsh*	Swedish punch (sweet liqueur)
sylt *sewlt*	jam
sås *soas*	sauce
sötningsmedel *surt·nihngs·mee·dehl*	artificial sweetener
sötpotatis *surt·poa·tah·tihs*	sweet potato
sötsur sås *surt·seur soas*	sweet-and-sour sauce
sött *suht*	sweet
T-benstek *tee·been·steek*	T-bone steak
thé *tee*	tea
timjan *tihm·yan*	thyme
toast skagen *toast skah·gehn*	toast with chopped shrimp in mayonnaise, topped with bleak roe
tomat *toa·maht*	tomato
tomater och lök *toa·mah·ter ohk lurk*	tomato and onion salad
tomatjuice *toa·maht·yoas*	tomato juice
tomatsoppa *toa·maht·soh·pa*	tomato soup

tomatsås *toa•maht•soas*	tomato sauce
tonfisk *toan•fihsk*	tuna
tonic *toh•nihk*	tonic water
torkade dadel *tohr•ka•der dah•dehl*	dried date
torkade fikon *tohr•ka•der fee•kohn*	dried fig
torrt *tohrt*	dry
torsk *torshk*	cod
tunga *tuhng•a*	tongue (cow)
tunn sås *tuhnn soas*	light (sauce)
tunnbröd *tuhnn•brurd*	Swedish flat bread, can be soft or crispy
tårta *toarta*	sponge-based fruit or cream cake
ugnsbakad fisk *eungns•bah•kad fihsk*	oven-baked fish
ugnsstekt kyckling *eungn•steekt chewk•lihng*	roast chicken
ugnsstekt potatis *eungn•steekt poa•tah•tihs*	roast potato
utan koffein *eu•tan ko•feen*	decaffeinated
vaktel *vak•tehl*	quail
valfria tillbehör *vahl•free•a tihl•beh•hurr*	choice of side dishes
valnöt *vahl•nurt*	walnut

vanilj *va·nihly*		vanilla
vaniljsås *va·nihly·soas*		vanilla sauce, often like custard
varmchoklad *varm shoa·klahd*		hot chocolate
varmkorv *varm kohrv*		hot dog
varmrätt *varm·rairt*		warm meal, usually main course
varmt *varmt*		hot
vatten *va·tehrn*		water
vattenkrasse *va·tehrn·kra·ser*		watercress
vaxböna *vax·bur·na*		butter bean
vegetarisk meny *vehg·eh·tah·risk meh·neu*		vegetarian menu
vermouth *vehr·meutt*		vermouth
vetemjöl *vee·teh·mjurl*		wheat flour (regular)
whisky *vihs·kee*		whisky
wienerbröd *vee·nehr·brurd*		Danish pastry
wienerschnitzel *vee·nehr·shniht·sehl*		breaded veal cutlet
vild champinjon *vihl·da sham·pihn·yoan*		wild mushroom
vildand *vihld·and*		wild duck
vilt *vihlt*		game
viltpastej *vihlt·pa·stay*		game pâté
vin *veen*		wine
vinaigrettesås *vih·neh·greht·soas*		vinaigrette [French dressing]
vinbär *veen·bair*		currant
vindruva *veen·dreu·va*		grape
vinlista *veen·lihs·ta*		wine list
vispgrädde *visp·greh·der*		whipped cream
vit sås *veet soas*		white sauce
vitkål *veet·koal*		white cabbage
vitkålssallad *veet·koal·sal·ad*		coleslaw
vitling *veet·lihng*		whiting

vitlök <u>veet</u>·l**ur**k	garlic
vitlöksmajonnäs <u>veet</u>·l**ur**ks·may·oa·<u>nairs</u>	garlic mayonnaise
vitlökssås <u>veet</u>·l**ur**k·s**oa**s	garlic sauce
vinbär <u>veen</u>·b**ai**r	currant
vindruva <u>veen</u>·dr**eu**·va	grape
vinlista <u>veen</u>·lihs·ta	wine list
vispgrädde <u>visp</u>·greh·der	whipped cream
vitt viht	white (wine)
vitt bröd viht br**ur**d	white bread
vodka <u>vod</u>·ka	vodka
vol au vent vohl·oa·<u>vahnt</u>	vol-au-vent (pastry filled with meat or fish)
våffla (med sylt och grädde) <u>vohf</u>·la meed sewlt ohk <u>greh</u>·der	waffle (with jam and whipped cream)
vårlök v**oa**r l**ur**k	shallot [spring onion]
västerbotten <u>vehs</u>·tehr·boh·tehn	strong, tangy, hard cheese
västkustsallad <u>vehst</u>·kuhst·<u>sal</u>·ad	west coast salad, with shrimp [prawns] and mussels
yoghurt <u>yoa</u>·geurt	yogurt
zucchini seu·<u>kee</u>·nee	zucchini [courgette]
ål **oa**l	eel

ångkokt fisk _oang_·koakt fisk	steamed fish
ädelost _air_·dehl·oast	blue cheese
ägg ehg	egg
äggplanta ehg·plan·ta	eggplant [aubergine]
äggula ehg·geu·la	egg yolk
äggröra ehg·rur·ra	scrambled egg
äggvita ehg·vee·ta	egg white
älg ehly	moose
älgfilé ehly·fih·_leh_	fillet of moose
älgstek ehly·steek	moose roast
älgstek med svampsås ehly·steek meed _svamp_·soas	roast moose with mushroom sauce
äppelkaka eh·pehl·_kah_·ka	apple cake
äppelpaj _ehp_·ehl·_pay_	apple tart
äppelring ehp·ehl·rihng	apple fritter
äpple _ehp_·leh	apple
ärta _air_·ta	pea
ärtsoppa _airt_·sohp·a	green or yellow pea soup
ättiksgurka _eh_·tihks·geur·ka	sweet, pickled gherkins
öl url	beer
öl på flaska url poa _fla_·ska	bottled beer

People

Conversation   115
Romance   121

ESSENTIAL

Hello!	**Hej!** *hay*
How are you?	**Hur står det till?** *heur stoar dee tihl*
Fine, thanks. And you?	**Bra, tack. Och du?** *brah tak ohk deu*
Excuse me!	**Ursäkta!** *eur·shehk·ta*
Do you speak English?	**Talar du engelska?** *tah·lar deu ehng·ehl·ska*
What's your name?	**Vad heter du?** *vahd hee·tehr deu*
My name is...	**Jag heter...** *yahg hee·tehr...*
Nice to meet you.	**Trevligt att träffas.** *treev·lihgt at trehf·as.*
Where are you from?	**Var kommer du ifrån?** *vahr ko·mehr deu ee·froan*
I'm from the U.S./U.K.	**Jag kommer från USA/Storbritannien.** *yahg koh·mehr froan eu ehs ah/stoap·bree·tan·yehn*
What do you do?	**Vad sysslar du med?** *vahd sews·lar deu meed*
I work for...	**Jag jobbar på.** *yahg yohb·ar poa...*
I'm a student.	**Jag är student.** *yahg air stuh·dent*
I'm retired.	**Jag är pensionär.** *yahg air pang·shoa·nair*
Do you like...?	**Tycker du om...?** *tew·kehr deu ohm...*
Goodbye.	**Hej då.** *hay·doa*
See you later.	**Vi ses.** *vee sees*

Language Difficulties

Do you speak English?	**Talar du engelska?** _tah·lar deu ehng·ehl·ska_
Does anyone here speak English?	**Talar någon engelska här?** _tah·lar noa·gohn ehng·ehl·ska hair_
I don't speak Swedish.	**Jag talar inte svenska.** _yahg tah·lar ihn·ter svehn·ska_
Could you speak more slowly?	**Kan du tala lite långsammare?** _kan deu tah·la lee·ter loang·sam·a·rer_
Could you repeat that?	**Kan du upprepa det?** _kan deu uhp·ree·pah dee_
Excuse me?	**Ursäkta?** _eur·shehk·ta_
What was that?	**Vad var det?** _vahd vahr dee_
Can you spell it?	**Kan du stava det?** _kahn deu stah·va deht_
Write it down, please.	**Skriv ner det, tack.** _skreev neer dee tak_
Can you translate this for me?	**Kan du översätta det här?** _kan deu ur·ver·seh·ta deet hair_
What does this/that mean?	**Vad betyder det här/där?** _vad beh·tew·der dee hair/dair_
I understand.	**Jag förstår.** _yahg furr·stoar_
I don't understand.	**Jag förstår inte.** _yahg furr·stoar ihn·ter_
Do you understand?	**Förstår du?** _furr·stoar deu_

YOU MAY HEAR...

Jag talar bara lite engelska. _yahg tah·lar bah·ra lee·ter ehng·ehl·ska_

I speak only a little English.

Jag talar inte engelska. _yahg tah·lar in·ter ehng·ehl·ska_

I don't speak English.

Swedes shake hands when greeting someone and when saying goodbye; this applies for meeting new people but is also often the case with colleagues or acquaintances. When you meet someone for the first time, shake hands and give your name. As in many countries, titles are more commonly used by the older generation, but you will sometimes hear **herr** (Mr.), **fru** (Mrs.) and **fröken** (Miss) used, as well as professional titles, e.g., **doktor** (doctor), **ingenjör** (engineer), etc.

Making Friends

Hello.	**Hej.** *hay*
Good morning.	**God morgon.** *goad <u>mor</u>•on*
Good afternoon.	**God middag.** *goad <u>mi</u>•dahg*
Good evening.	**God afton.** *goad <u>af</u>•tohn*
My name is…	**Jag heter…** *yahg <u>hee</u>•tehr…*
What's your name?	**Vad heter du?** *vahd <u>hee</u>•tehr deu*
I'd like to introduce you to…	**Får jag presentera…** *foar yahg preh•sehn•<u>tee</u>•ra…*
Pleased to meet you.	**Trevligt att träffas.** *<u>treev</u>•lihgt at <u>treh</u>•fas*

How are you?	**Hur står det till?** *heur stoar dee tihl*
Fine, thanks.	**Bra, tack.** *brah tak*
And you?	**Och du?** *ohk deu*

Travel Talk

I'm here...	**Jag är här...** *yahg air hair...*
on business	**på affärsresa** *poa a-fairs-ree-sa*
on vacation [holiday]	**på semester** *poa seh-mehs-tehr*
studying	**för studier** *furr steu-de-ehr*
I'm staying for...	**Jag ska stanna i...** *yahg skah sta-na ee...*
I've been here..	**Jag har varit här i...** *yahg hahr vah-riht hair ee...*
a day	**en dag** *ehn dahg*
a week	**en vecka** *ehn veh-ka*
a month	**en månad** *ehn moa-nad*
Where are you from?	**Var kommer du ifrån?** *vahr koh-mehr deu ee-froan*
I'm from.	**Jag kommer från.** *yahg koh-mehr froan...*

For Numbers, see page 179.

Personal

Who are you here with?	**Vem är du här med?** *vehm air deu hair meed*
I'm on my own.	**Jag är ensam.** *yahg air ehn-sam*
I'm with...	**Jag är här med...** *yahg air hair meed...*
my husband/wife	**min man/fru** *mihn man/freu*
my boyfriend	**min pojkvän** *mihn povk-vehn*
girlfriend	**flickvän** *flihk-vehn*
a friend/friends	**en vän/vänner** *ehn vehn/venhn-ehr*
a colleague	**en kollega** *ehn koh-lee-ga/*
colleagues	**kolleger** *koh-lee-goahr*
When's your birthday?	**När fyller du år?** *nair fewl-ehr deu oar*

How old are you?	**Hur gammal är du?** _heur gah·mal air deu_
I'm...	**Jag är...** _yahg air..._
single	**ogift** _oa·yift_
in a relationship	**i ett förhållande** _ee eht furr·hoal·an·der_
engaged	**förlovad** _fuhr·loh·vad_
married	**gift** _yihft_
divorced	**skild** _shihld_
separated	**separerad** _seh·pa·ree·rad_
I'm a widow/widower.	**Jag är änka/änkling.** _yahg air ehng·ka/ehnak·lihna_
Do you have children/ grandchildren?	**Har du barn/barnbarn?** _hahr deu bahrn/bahrn·bahrn_

For Numbers, see page 179.

Work & School

What do you do?	**Vad sysslar du med?** _vahd sews·lar deu meed_
What are you studying?	**Vad läser du?** _vahd lai·sehr deu_
I'm studying...	**Jag läser...** _yahg lai·sehr..._
I work full time/ part time.	**Jag arbetar heltid/deltid.** _yahg ahr·beh·tar hehl·teed/dehl·teed_
I work at home.	**Jag arbetar hemifrån.** _yahg ahr·beh·tar hehm·ih·froan_
I'm unemployed	**Jag är arbetslös.** _yahg air ar·behts·lus_
Who do you work for?	**Vilken firma jobbar du på?** _vihl·kehn fihr·ma yohb·ar deu poa_
I work for...	**Jag jobbar på...** _yahg yohb·ar poa..._
Here's my business card.	**Här är mitt kort.** _hair air miht koahrt_

For Business Travel, see page 155.

Weather

What's the weather forecast for tomorrow?	**Vad är väderleksrapporten för imorgon?** *vahd air vair•dehr•leeks•ra•pohr•tehn furr ee•mo•ron*
What beautiful/ terrible weather!	**Vilket vackert/förskräckligt väder!** *vihl•keht va•kert/furr•skrehk•ligt vair•dehr*
It's...	**Det är...** *dee air...*
hot/cold	**varmt/kallt** *varmt/kahlt*
cool/warm	**svalt/varmt** *svahlt/varmt*
rainy/sunny	**regnigt/soligt** *rehng•nihkt/soal•ikt*
snowy/icy	**snöigt/halt** *snur•ikt/hahlt*
Do I need a jacket/ an umbrella?	**Behöver jag en jacka/ett paraply?** *beh•hur•ver yahg ehn yah•ka/eht pa•ra•plew*

For Temperature, see page 186.

ESSENTIAL

Would you like to go out for a drink/dinner?	**Har du lust att ta en drink/gå ut och äta?** *hahr deu luhst at tah ehn drihnk/goa eut ohk air·ta*
What are your plans for tonight/tomorrow?	**Vad har du för planer för ikväll/imorgon?** *vahd hahr deu furr plah·nehr furr ee·kvehl/ee·mo·ron*
Can I have your number?	**Kan jag få ditt telefonnummer?** *kan yahg foa diht teh·leh·foan·nuhm·ehr*
May I join you?	**Får jag göra dig sällskap?** *foar yahg yurra dihg sehl·skahp*
Can I buy you a drink?	**Får jag bjuda på en drink?** *foar yahg byeu·da poa ehn drihnk*
I like you.	**Jag gillar dig.** *yahg yihi·ar day*
I love you.	**Jag älskar dig.** *yahg ehl·skar day*

The Dating Game

Would you like to…?	**Har du lust att…?** *hahr deu luhst at…*
go out for coffee	**gå ut och ta en kopp kaffe** *goa eut ohk tah ehn kohp ka·fer*
go for a drink	**ta en drink** *tah ehn drihnk*
go out for a meal	**gå ut och äta** *goa eut ohk air·ta*
What are your plans for…?	**Vad har du för planer för…?** *vahd hahr deu furr plah·nehr furr…*
today	**idag** *ee·dahg*
tonight	**ikväll** *ee·kvehl*
tomorrow	**imorgon** *ee·mo·ron*
this weekend	**den här helgen** *dehn hair hehl·yehn*
Where would you like to go?	**Vart vill du gå?** *vart vihl deu goa*

I'd like to go to...	**Jag skulle vilja gå till.** *yahg skuh•ler vihl•ya* *goa tihl...*
Do you like...?	**Tycker du om...?** *tew•kehr deu ohm...*
Can I have your number/e-mail?	**Kan jag få ditt nummer/din e-post?** *kan yahg foa diht nuhm•ehr/dihn ee•pohst*
Are you on Facebook/ Twitter?	**Finns du på Facebook/Twitter?** *fihns deu poa Facebook/Twitter*
Can I join you?	**Får jag följa med?** *foar yahg furl•ya meed*
You're very attractive.	**Du är väldigt snygg.** *deu air vehl•dihkt snewgg*
You look great!	**Vad du ser vacker ut!** *vahd deu seer va•kehr eut*
Shall we go somewhere quieter?	**Ska vi gå till ett lugnare ställe?** *skah vee* *goa tihl eht luhng•na•rer stehl•ler*

For Communications, see page 49.

Accepting & Rejecting

Thank you. I'd love to.	**Tack, det vill jag gärna.** *tak dee vihl yahg yair•na*
Where should we meet?	**Var ska vi träffas?** *vahr skah vee treh•fas*
I'll meet you at the bar/your hotel.	**Vi träffas i baren/på ditt hotell.** *vee treh•fas* *ee bahr•en/poa diht hoh•tehl*
I'll come by at...	**Jag kommer...** *yahg koh•mehr...*

What's your address?	**Vilken address har du?** *Vihl·kehn ahd·rehs hahr deu*
Thank you,	**Tack, men jag är upptagen.** *tak men yahg*
but I'm busy.	*air uhp·tah·gehn*
I'm not interested.	**Jag är inte intresserad.** *yahg air in·ter in·treh·see·rad*
Leave me alone,	**Kan du lämna mig ifred, tack!** *kan deu*
please!	*lehm·na may ee·freed tak*
Stop bothering me!	**Sluta störa mig!** *sluh·ta stur·ra may*

Getting Intimate

Can I hug/kiss you?	**Får jag krama/kysa dig?** *foar yahg krah·ma/*
	chews·a day
Yes.	**Ja.** *yah*
No.	**Nej.** *nay*
Stop!	**Stopp!** *stop*

Sexual Preferences

Are you gay?	**Är du gay?** *air deu gay*
I'm...	**Jag är...** *yahg air...*
heterosexual	**heterosexuell** *heh·tehr·ro·sehk·shew·ehl*
homosexual	**homosexuell** *hoh·moa·sehk·shew·ehl*
bisexual	**bisexuell** *bee·sehk·shew·ehl*
Do you like men/	**Gillar du män/kvinnor?** *yih·lahr deu mehn/*
women?	*kvih·nohr*

For Grammar, see page 175.

Leisure Time

Sightseeing	125
Shopping	129
Sport & Leisure	144
Going Out	151

ESSENTIAL

Where's the tourist information office?	**Var ligger turistinformationen?** *vahr lih·gehr teu·rihst·ihn·fohr·ma·shoan·ehn*
What are the main points of interest?	**Vad finns det för sevärdheter?** *vahd fihns dee furr see·vaird·hee·tehr*
Do you have tours in English?	**Finns det några turer på engelska?** *fihns dee noa·gra teu·rehr poa ehng·ehl·ska*
Can I have a map/ guide, please?	**Kan jag få en karta/guide, tack?** *kan yahg foa ehn kahr·ta/gujd tak*

Tourist Information

Do you have any information on…?	**Har ni information om…?** *hahr nee ihn·for·ma·shoan om…*
Can you recommend…?	**Kan ni rekommendera…?** *kan nee reh·koh·mehn dee·ra…*
a boat trip	**en båttur** *ehn boat·teur*
an excursion	**en rundtur** *ehn ruhnd·teur*
a sightseeing tour	**en sightseeingtur** *ehn sight·see·ihng·teur*

On Tour

I'd like to go on the tour to…	**Jag vill följa med på turen till…** *yahg vihl furl·ja meed poa teu·ren tihl…*
When's the next tour?	**När går nästa rundresa?** *nair goar nehsta ruhnd·rehsa*
Are there tours in English?	**Finns det någon tur på engelska?** *fihns dee noa·gohn teur poa ehng·ehl·ska*

There are tourist information offices in all large cities and towns. These are usually marked by a green sign with an **I**. For general information, Sweden's official tourism website is a good place to start. Here you can find information on accommodation, attractions and activities as well as cultural and historical information. Most cities have their own tourist boards and websites, where you can request brochures, maps and more prior to your arrival. Also look for **Stockholmskortet** (the Stockholm Card) if you will be spending several days in the city. For one fee, you have access to musems, events and transportation throughout the city. You can choose whether you want the card for 24, 48 or 72 hours. The equivalent in Göteborg is **Göteborgs Passet.**

Is there an English-speaking guide/audio guide?	**Finns det en engelsktalande guide/ljudguide?** *fihns deht ehn ehng•ehlsk•tah•lan•de gahyd/ aw•dee•oh gahyd*
What time do we leave/return?	**När åker vi/kommer vi tillbaka?** *nair <u>oa</u>k•er vee/<u>koh</u>•mehr vee tihl•<u>bah</u>•ka*
We'd like to have a look at...	**Vi skulle vilja se...** *vee <u>skuh</u>•ler <u>vihl</u>•ya see...*
Can we stop here...?	**Kan vi stanna här...?** *kan vee <u>sta</u>•na hair...*
to take photographs	**för att ta foton** *furr at tah <u>foa</u>•tohn*
to buy souvenirs	**för att köpa souvenirer** *furr at <u>chur</u>•pa seu•veh•<u>nee</u>•rehr*
to use the toilets	**för att gå på toaletten** *furr at goa poa toa•ah•<u>leh</u>•tehn*
Is there access for the disabled?	**Finns det tillgång för rörelsehindrade?** *fihns dee tihl•<u>goa</u>ng furr <u>rurr</u>•ehl•ser•<u>hihn</u>•dra•der*

For Tickets, see page 21.

Seeing the Sights

Where is…?	**Var ligger…?** *vahr <u>lih</u>•gehr…*
the battleground	**slagfältet** *<u>slahg</u>•fehl•teht*
the botanical garden	**botaniska trädgården** *boa•<u>tan</u>•ihs•ska <u>traird</u>•goar•dehn*
Where is…?	**Var ligger…?** *vahr <u>lih</u>•gehr…*
the castle	**slottet** *<u>sloht</u>•eht*
the downtown area	**centrum** *<u>sehn</u>•truhm*
the fountain	**fontänen** *fohn•<u>tairn</u>•ehn*
the library	**biblioteket** *bihb•lee•oa•<u>teek</u>•eht*
the market	**torget** *<u>tohr</u>•yeht*
the museum	**museet** *muh•<u>see</u>•eht*
the old town	**gamla stan** *<u>gam</u>•la stahn*
the opera house	**operan** *oap•eh•ran*
the palace	**slottet** *<u>sloht</u>•eht*
the park	**parken** *<u>park</u>•ehn*
the shopping area	**Et affärscentrumet** *eht a•<u>ffairs</u>•sehn•truhm•eht*
the town hall	**stadshuset** *<u>stads</u>•heus•eht*
Can you show me on the map?	**Kan du visa mig på kartan?** *kan deu vee•sa may poa <u>kahr</u>•tan*
It's…	**Det är…** *det air…*
amazing	**fantastiskt** *fan•ta•stihskt*
beautiful	**vackert** *<u>va</u>•kehrt*
boring	**trist** *trihst*
interesting	**intressant** *in•treh•<u>sant</u>*
magnificent	**storslaget** *<u>stoar</u>•slahg•eht*
romantic	**romantiskt** *roh•<u>man</u>•tihskt*
strange	**konstigt** *kohn•stihgt*
stunning	**förbluffande** *furr•bluh•fahnder*

terrible	**hemskt** *hehmskt*
ugly	**fult** *feult*
I (don't) like it.	**Jag tycker (inte) om den/det.** *yahg <u>tew</u>•kehr (<u>in</u>•ter) ohm dehn/d**ee***

For Asking Directions, see page 35.

For Grammar, see page 175.

Religious Sites

Where is…?	**Var är…?** *vahr air…*
the cathedral	**domkyrkan** *dohm•chewr•kahn*
the church	**kyrkan** <u>chewr</u>•kan
the mosque	**moskén** *mos•<u>kehn</u>*
the shrine	**altaret** <u>alt</u>•a•reht
the synagogue	**synagogan** *sihn•a•<u>gohg</u>•an*
the temple	**templet** <u>tehmp</u>•leht
What time is mass/ the service?	**Hur dags är mässan/gudstjänsten?** *heur daks air <u>mehs</u>•an/<u>geuds</u>•tjain•stehn*

Shopping

ESSENTIAL

Where is the market/ mall [shopping centre]?	**Var ligger orget/affärscentrumet?** *vahr lih·gehr tohr·yeht/a·ffairs·sehn·truhm·eht*
I'm just looking.	**Jag tittar bara.** *yahg tih·tar bah·ra*
Can you help me?	**Kan du hjälpa mig?** *kan deu yehlp·a may*
I'm being helped.	**Jag får hjälp, tack.** *yahg foar yehlp tak*
How much does it cost?	**Hur mycket kostar det?** *heur mew·ker kos·tar det*
This/That one, thanks.	**Den här/där, tack.** *dehn hair/dair tak*
That's all, thanks.	**Det var allt, tack.** *dee vahr alt tak*
Where do I pay?	**Var kan jag betala?** *vahr kan yahg beh·tah·la*
I'll pay in cash/by credit card.	**Jag vill betala kontant/med kreditkort.** *yahg vihl beh·tah·la kohn·tant/meed kreh·deet·koart*
A receipt, please.	**Kvittot, tack.** *kvih·tot tak*

At the Shops

Where is...?	**Var finns...?** *vahr fihns...*
the antiques store	**antikaffären** *an·teek·a·ffair·ehn*
the bakery	**bageriet** *bahg·eh·ree·eht*
the bookstore	**bokhandeln** *boak·han·dehln*
the clothing store	**klädaffären** *klaird·a·ffair·ehn*
the delicatessen	**delikatessaffären** *dehl·eh·ka·tehs·a·fair·ehn*
the department store	**varuhuset** *vahr·eu·heus·eht*
the health food store	**hälsokostaffären** *hehl·soa·kost·a·fair·ehn*

the jeweler	**juveleraren** *yeu·veh·lee·rar·ehn*
the liquor store [off licence]	**systembolaget** *sews·teem·boa·lahg·eht*
the market	**torget** *tohr·yeht*
the pastry shop	**konditoriet** *kohn·deh·toh·ree·eht*
the pharmacy [chemist]	**apoteket** *a·poa·tee·keht*
the produce [grocery] store	**livsmedelsaffären** *lihvs·mee·dehls·a·fair·ehn*
the shoe store	**skoaffären** *skoa·a·fair·ehn*
the shopping mall [shopping centre]	**affärscentrumet** *a·ffairs·sehn·truhm·eht*
the souvenir store	**souvenirbutiken** *seu·veh·neer·buh·tee·kehn*
the supermarket	**snabbköpet** *snab·chur·peht*

Although Sweden still has many small, specialty shops, **Köpcentrum** (malls) are becoming more and more common, especially in larger towns. Many chain and department stores, such as **Åhléns** and **Kappahl** and **Hennes & Mauritz**, have branches all over the country, all of which sell quality goods. In the well-established Stockholm department store **NK**, you can find almost anything, though it can be quite expensive. Designer goods can be found at **DesignTorget** in Stockholm. For traditional handicrafts look for signs with **hemslöjd** (handicraft); in Stockholm, these can be found at **Svensk Hemslöjd** and **Svenskt Hantverk** (traditional handicraft stores). Many towns have colorful markets, where you can buy anything from fresh fruit and vegetables to flowers and handicrafts. **Julmarknaden** (Christmas market) in Stockholm in the Old Town and **Skansen** (outdoor park and museum), are historic shopping areas.

Where is…?	**Var finns…?** *vahr fihns…*
the tobacconist	**tobaksaffären** *toa·baks·a·ffair·ehn*
the toy store	**leksaksaffären** *leek·sahks·a·fair·ehn*

Ask an Assistant

When do you open/ close?	**När öppnar/stänger ni?** *nair uhp·nar/ stehng·er nee*
Where is…?	**Var finns…?** *vahr fihns…*
the cashier [cash desk]	**kassan** *kah·san*
the escalator	**rulltrappan** *ruhl·tra·pan*
the elevator [lift]	**hissen** *his·ehn*
the fitting room	**provrummet** *proav·ruhm·eht*
the store directory [guide]	**informationen** *in·for·ma·shoa·nehn*
Can you help me?	**Kan du hjälpa mig?** *kan deu yehl·pa may*
I'm just looking.	**Jag tittar bara.** *yahg tih·tar bah·ra*
I'm being helped.	**Tack, jag får hjälp.** *tak yahg foar yehlp*
Do you have any…?	**Har ni några…?** *hahr nee noa·gra…*
Could you show me…?	**Kan du visa mig några…?** *kan deu vee·sa may noa·gra…*

YOU MAY HEAR...

Kan jag hjälpa er? *kan yahg yehl•pa her* — Can I help you?
Ett ögonblick, tack. *eht ur•gohn•blihk tak* — Just a moment, please.
Vad vill ni beställa? *vahd vihl nee beh•steh•la* — What would you like?
Något annat? *noa•goht an•nat* — Anything else?

Can you ship/wrap it?	**Kan du skicka/slå in det?** *kan deu shih•ka dee/ sloa ihn dee*
How much does it cost?	**Hur mycket kostar det?** *heur mew•kerht kos•tar dee*
That's all, thanks.	**Det var allt, tack.** *dee vahr alt tak*

For Clothes & Accessories, see page 138.

For Meals & Cooking, see page 65.

Personal Preferences

I want something...	**Jag skulle vilja ha något...** *yahg skuh•ler vihl•ya hah noa•goht...*
cheap/expensive	**billigt/dyrt** *bihl•igt/dewyt*

YOU MAY SEE...

ÖPPET/STÄNGT	open/closed
STÄNGT FÖR LUNCH	closed for lunch
PROVRUM	fitting room
KASSÖR/KASSÖRSKA	cashier
ENDAST KONTANT	cash only
VI TAR KREDITKORT	credit cards accepted
AFFÄRSTID	business hours
UTGÅNG	exit

larger/smaller	**större/mindre** _sturr•er/mihn•drer_	
from this region	**från denna region** _frohn deh•na regheoan_	
Is it real?	**Är den äkta?** _air dehn aik•ta_	
Could you show me this/that?	**Kan du visa mig den här/där?** _kan deu vee•sa may dehn hair/dair_	
That's not quite what I want.	**Det är inte riktigt vad jag vill ha.** _dee air ihn•ter rihk•tikt vahd yahg vihl hah_	
I don't like it.	**Jag tycker inte om det.** _yahg tew•kehr ihn•ter ohm dee_	
That's too expensive.	**Det är för dyrt.** _dee air furr dewrt_	
I'd like to think about it.	**Jag behöver tänka på det.** _Yahg beh•hur•vehr tehng•ka poa dee_	
I'll take it.	**Jag tar den.** _yahg tahr dehn_	

Paying & Bargaining

How much does it cost?	**Hur mycket kostar det?** _heur mew•ker kos•tar dee_	
I'll pay…	**Jag betalar…** _yahg beh•tah•lar…_	
in cash	**kontant** _kohn•tant_	
by credit card	**med kreditkort** _meed kreh•deet•koart_	
by traveler's check [cheque]	**med en resecheck** _meed ehn ree•seh•shehk_	
The receipt, please.	**Kvittot, tack.** _kvih•toht tak_	
That's too much.	**Det är för mycket.** _dee air furr mew•ker_	
I'll give you…	**Jag kan ge er…** _yahg kan yee ehr…_	
I only have…kronor.	**Jag har bara…kronor.** _yahg hahr bah•ra…kroa•nohr_	
Is that your best price?	**Är det ditt bästa pris?** _air deht diht beh•sta prihs_	
Can you give me a discount?	**Kan du ge mig rabatt?** _kan deu yee may ra•bat_	

For Numbers, see page 179.

YOU MAY HEAR...

Hur vill ni betala? *heur vihl nee beh·tah·la* | How are you paying?

Ditt kreditkort har avvisats. | Your credit card has
diht kreh·dith·koart hahr ahv·veesahts | been declined.

ID, tack. *ee·deh, tak.* | ID, please.

Vi tar inte kreditkort. | We don't accept
Vee tahr ihnte kreh·diht·koart | credit cards.

Bara kontanter, tack. | Cash only, please.
bah·ra kohn·tan·tehr tak

Har du mindre växel? *hahr deu mihn·drer* | Do you have any
vehx·ehl | smaller change?

Making a Complaint

I'd like...	**Jag skulle vilja...** *yahg skuh·ler vihl·ya...*
to exchange this	**byta den här** *bew·ta dehn hair*
to return this	**återlämna den här** *oa·tehr·lehm·na dehn hair*
a refund	**ha pengarna tillbaka** *hah pehng·ar·na tihl·bah·ka*
to see the manager	**få träffa butikschefen** *foa treh·fa beu·teeks·sheef·ehn*

Services

Can you recommend...?	**Kan du rekommendera...?** *kan deu reh·koh·mehn·dee·ra...*
a barber	**en herrfrisör** *ehn hair·fri·surr*
a dry cleaner	**en kemtvätt** *ehn shehm·tveht*
a hairdresser	**en damfrisör** *ehn dahm·free·surr*
a laundromat [launderette]	**en snabbtvätt** *ehn snab·tveht*
a nail salon	**en nagelvårdssalong** *ehn nah·gehl·voards·sa·loang*

a spa	**ett spa** *eht spah*
a travel agency	**en resebyrå** *ehn ree·seh·bew·roa*
Can you…this?	**Kan ni…den här?** *kan nee…dehn hair*
alter	**ändra på** *ehn·dra poa*
clean	**göra ren** *yur·ra reen*
mend	**laga** *lah·ga*
press	**stryka** *strew·ka*
When will it be ready?	**När blir det klart?** *nair bleer dee klahrt*

Hair & Beauty

I'd like…	**Jag vill…** *yahg vihl…*
an appointment for today/ tomorrow	**boka en tid till idag/imorgon** *boa·ka ehn teed tihl ee·dahg/ee·mo·ron*
some colour/ highlights	**färg/slingor** *fehry/slihng·ohr*
my hair styled/ blow-dried	**få en ny frisyr/föning** *foa ehn new free·sewr/ funeeng*
a hair cut	**få en klippning** *foa ehn klihp·nihng*
an eyebrow/ a bikini wax	**en vaxning av ögonbrynen/bikinilinjen** *ehn vaks·nihng afv ur·gonn·brew·nehn/ beh·kee·nee·leen·yehn*
a facial	**en ansiktsbehandling** *ehn an·sihkts·beh·hand·lihng*

Spas and wellness centers are becoming increasingly popular.
There are many to choose from, both in urban and rural areas.
It is possible to find spas that offer everything from traditional
massage, such as the Swedish massage, which focuses on circulation
and relaxation, to yoga, exercise and more. Some are even eco-friendly.
Many spas and health centers also have gyms, pools and saunas.

a manicure/ pedicure	**en manikyr/pedikyr** *ehn ma·nee·kewr/ pehd·ee·kewr*	
a (sports) massage	**(tränings) massage** *(trair·nihngs·) ma·sahsh*	
a trim, please...	**en klippning, tack...** *ehn klihp·nihng, tak*	
Don't cut it too short.	**Klipp det inte för kort.** *klihp dee ihn·ter furr koart*	
Shorter here.	**Kortare här.** *koar·ta·rer hair*	
Do you do...?	**Ger ni...?** *yehr nee...*	
acupuncture	**akupunktur** *a·keu·puhnk·teur*	
aromatherapy	**aroma-terapi** *a·roa·ma·teh·ra·pee*	
oxygen treatment	**syrebehandling** *sew·reh·beh·hand·lihng*	
Is there a sauna?	**Finns det bastu?** *fihns dee bas·teu*	

Antiques

How old is this?	**Hur gammalt är det här?** *heur gam·alt air dee hair*
Do you have anything from the ... era?	**Har ni något från ... perioden?** *hahr nee noh·goht frohn ... per·eeoh·dehn*
Will I have problems with customs?	**Får jag problem i tullen?** *foar yahg proa·bleem ee tuh·lehn*
Is there a certificate of authenticity?	**Finns det ett äkthetsbevis?** *fihns dee eht ehkt·heets·beh·vees*
Can you ship/wrap it?	**Kan ni skicka/packa in det?** *kahn nee shih·ka/ paka ihn deht*

Clothing

I'd like...	**Jag skulle vilja ha...** *yahg skuh·ler vihl·ya hah...*
Can I try this on?	**Kan jag prova den här?** *kan yahg proa·va dehn hair*

YOU MAY SEE...

HERRKLÄDER	men's clothing
DAMKLÄDER	women's clothing
BARNKLÄDER	children's clothing

YOU MAY HEAR...

Du klär jättebra i den. *Deu klair jai·teh·brah i dehn* — That looks great on you.

Hur sitter den? *huhr sih·tehr dehn* — How does it fit?

Vi har inte din storlek. *Vee hahr ihnte deen stohr·lehk* — We don't have your size.

It doesn't fit.	**Den passar inte.** *dehn pas·ar ihn·ter*	
It's too...	**Den är för...** *dehn air furr...*	
big	**stor** *stoar*	
small	**liten** *lee·tehn*	
short	**kort** *kort*	
long	**lång** *loang*	
tight	**liten** *leetehn*	
loose	**stor** *stohr*	
Do you have this in size...?	**Har ni den här i storlek...?** *hahr nee dehn hair ee stoar·leek...*	
Do you have this in a bigger/smaller size?	**Har ni den här i en större/en mindre storlek?** *hahr nee dehn hair ee ehn stur·re/ ehn mihn·drer stoar·leek*	

For Numbers, see page 179.

Colors

I'm looking for something in...	**Jag söker något i...** *yahg sur·ker noa·goht ee...*	
beige	**beige** *beesh*	
black	**svart** *svart*	
blue	**blått** *bloat*	

brown	**brunt** *breunt*
gray	**grått** *groat*
green	**grönt** *grurnt*
orange	**orange** *oa·ransh*
pink	**rosa** *roa·sa*
purple	**lila** *lee·la*
red	**rött** *ruhrt*
white	**vitt** *vit*
yellow	**gult** *geult*
I'm looking for something in…	**Jag söker något i…** *yahg sur·ker noa·goht ee…*

Clothes & Accessories

a backpack	**ryggsäck** *rewg·sehk*
a belt	**skärp** *shairp*
a bikini	**bikini** *bih·kee·nee*
a blouse	**blus** *bleus*
a bra	**behå** *beh·hoa*
briefs [underpants]	**kalsonger [underbyxor]** *khal·sohn·gehr [uhn·dehr·bew·xohr]*
panties	**trosor** *troh·sohr*
a coat	**rock** *rohk*
a dress	**klänning** *klehn·ihng*
a hat	**hatt** *hat*
a jacket	**jacka** *ya·ka*
jeans	**jeans** *jeens*
pajamas	**pyjamas** *pew·ya·mas*
pants [trousers]	**byxor** *bewx·ohr*
panty hose [tights]	**strumpbyxor** *struhmp·bewx·ohr*
a purse [handbag]	**handväska** *hand·vehs·ka*
a raincoat	**regnkappa** *rehngn·kap·a*

a scarf	**halsduk** _hals_•_deuk_
a shirt	**skjorta** _shoar_•ta
shorts	**shorts** _shohrts_
a skirt	**kjol** _choal_
socks	**sockar** _soh_•kar
stockings	**strumpor** _stuhm_•pohr
a suit (jacket and pants)	**kostym** kos•_tewm_
a suit (jacket and skirt)	**dräkt** _drehkt_
sunglasses	**solglasögon** _soal_•glahs•**_ur_**•gohn
a sweater	**tröja** _trur_•ya
a sweatshirt	**sweatshirt** _sweat_•shirt swimming
swimming trunks	**badbyxor** _bahd_•bewx•ohr
a swimsuit	**baddräkt** _bahd_•drehkt
a T-shirt	**T-skjorta** _tee_•shoarta
a tie	**slips** _slihps_
underpants (men's/women's)	**kalsonger/trosor** kal•_soang_•ehr/_troa_•sohr
underwear	**underkläder** uhn•dehr•_klai_•dehr

Fabric

I'd like…	**Jag skulle vilja ha…** yahg _skuh_•ler _vihl_•ya hah…
cotton	**bomull** _boam_•uhl
denim	**denim** _dehn_•ihm
lace	**spets** _spehts_
leather	**läder** _lair_•der
linen	**linne** _lih_•ner
silk	**siden** _see_•dehn
wool	**ull** _uhl_
Is it machine washable?	**Kan det tvättas i maskin?** kan dee _tveht_•as ee ma•_sheen_

Shoes

I'd like...	**Jag skulle vilja ha...** *yahg skuh•ler vihl•ya hah...*
high-heeled/	**högklackade/lågklackade skor**
flat shoes	*hurg•klak•a•der/loag•klak•a•der skoar*
boots	**stövlar** *stuhv•lar*
I'd like...	**Jag skulle vilja ha...** *yahg skuh•ler vihl•ya hah...*
loafers	**loafers** *loa•fers*
sandals	**sandaler** *san•dahl•ehr*
shoes	**skor** *skoar*
slippers	**tofflor** *toff•lohr*
sneakers	**träningsskor** *trair•nihngs•skoar*
In size...	**I storlek...** *ee stoar•leek...*

For Numbers, see page 179.

Sizes

Small (S)	**liten** *leet•ehn*
Medium (M)	**medium** *mee•dee•uhm*
large (L)	**stor** *stoar*
extra large (XL)	**extra stor** *ehx•tra stoar*
petite	**petite** *peh•teet*
plus size	**plus-storlek** *pleus•stoar•leek*

Newsagent & Tobacconist

Do you sell English language books/ newspapers?	**Säljer ni böcker/tidningar på engelska?** *sehl•yehr nee bur•kehr/teed•nihng•ar poa ehng•ehl•ska*
I'd like...	**Jag skulle vilja ha...** *yahg skuh•ler vihl•ya hah...*
candy [sweets]	**godis [sötsaker]** *goa•dihs [sut•sahk•ehr]*
some chewing gum	**tuggummi** *tuhg•guh•mee*
a chocolate bar	**en chokladkaka** *ehn shohk•lahd•kahka*
some cigars	**några cigarrer** *noa•gra see•gahr•er*
a pack/carton of cigarettes	**ett paket/en limpa cigaretter** *eht pak•eht/ ehn lihm•pa sih•ga•reht•her*
a lighter	**en tändare** *ehn tehn•da•rehr*
a magazine	**en veckotidning** *ehn veh•koa•teed•nihng*
matches	**tändstickor** *tehnd•stik•ohr*
a newspaper	**en tidning** *ehn teed•nihng*
a pen	**en penna** *ehn peh•na*
a postcard	**ett vykort** *eht vew•koart*
a road/town map of...	**en vägkarta/stadskarta över...** *ehn vairg•kahr•ta/stats•kahr•ta ur•vehr...*
some stamps	**några frimärken** *noa•gra free•mair•kehn*

Photography

I'm looking for... camera.	**Jag skulle vilja köpa...kamera.** *yahg skuh•ler vihl•ya chur•pa... kah•meh•ra*
an automatic	**en automatisk** *ehn ah•toa•mah•tihsk*
a digital	**en digital** *ehn dih•gih•tahl*
a disposable	**en engångs** *ehn een•goangs*
I'd like...	**Jag skulle vilja ha...** *yahg skuh•ler vihl•ya hah...*
a battery	**ett batteri** *eht ba•teh•ree*
a digital print	**ett digitalt kort** *eht dih•gih•tahlt koart*
a memory card	**ett minneskort** *eht mihn•ehs•koart*

| Can I print digital photos here? | **Kan jag skriva ut digitala foton här?** *kan yahg skree•va eut dih•gih•tah•la foh•toan hair* |

Souvenirs

candlesticks	**ljusstakar** *yeus•stah•kar*
Christmas decorations	**juldekorationer** *yeul•dehk•oh•ra•shoan•ehr*
clogs	**träskor** *trair•skoar*
crystal (glass)	**kristallglas** *kree•stal•glahs*
a Dala horse (red wooden horse)	**en dalahäst** *ehn dah•la•hehst*
dolls	**dockor** *dok•oar*
glassware	**glasföremål** *glahs•furr•reh•moal*
handicrafts	**hemslöjd** *hehm•sluhyd*
horn work	**något i horn** *noa•goht ee hoarn*
jewelry	**smycken** *smew•kehn*
porcelain	**porslin** *pohrsh•leen*
pottery	**keramik** *cheh•ra•meek*
reindeer antlers	**renhorn** *reen•hoarn*
Sami handicrafts	**sameslöjd** *sah•meh•sluhyd*
smoked salmon	**rökt lax** *rurkt lax*
a tablecloth	**en duk** *ehn deuk*
textiles	**textil** *tehx•teel*
wood carvings	**träfigurer** *trair•fih•geu•rehr*
a wooden knife	**en träkniv** *ehn trair•kneev*
a wooden spoon	**en träsked** *ehn trair•sheed*
Can I see this/that?	**Får jag se på den här/där?** *foar yahg she poa dehn hair/dair*
The one in the window/display case.	**Den i fönstret/vitrinet.** *dehn ee furn•streht/vi•treen•eht*
I'd like…	**Jag skulle vilja ha…** *yahg skuh•ler vihl•ya hah…*
a battery	**ett batteri** *eht ba•teh•ree*

a bracelet	**ett armband**	eht _arm_·band
a brooch	**en brosch**	ehn broash
earrings	**örhängen**	_ur_·hehng·ehn
a necklace	**ett halsband**	eht _hals_·band
a ring	**en ring**	ehn rihng
a watch	**en armbandsklocka**	ehn _arm_·bands·_kloh_·ka
copper	**koppar**	_kohpp_·ar

When it comes to souvenirs, whether you are looking for something traditional or modern, you are sure to find just the thing in Sweden. **Träslöjd** (woodwork), **hemslöjd** (handicrafts), **keramik** (ceramics) and Swedish crystal are popular, traditional souvenirs. The **dalahäst** (Dala horse) is perhaps one of the most famous and ubiquitous souvenirs; traditionally, its color is a reddish-orange, but the horses can now be found in a wide range of colors and sizes. Sweden is known for its design, which is evident in its selection of **porslin** (fine china) and ceramics. Some well-known manufacturers include **Höganäs Keramik** and **Rörstrand**, the latter being the second oldest porcelain manufacturer in Europe, founded in 1746. Sweden is also famous for its glass and crystal, both with respect to design and to quality. **Glasriket** (the kingdom of glass) located in Småland, in southeastern Sweden, has around 15 glass factories, including some of the most famous glassworks in Sweden, such as **Kosta Boda**, **Orrefors** and **Nybro**. Factory tours are often available. In addition to the traditional Swedish handicrafts mentioned above, **sameslöjd** (Sámi handicraft) is something that should not be overlooked. The **Sámi** are known for their beautiful crafts, which include jewelry and knives carved from reindeer antlers, jewelry made from beaded pewter and reindeer leather as well as a wide range of clothing in reindeer leather and different types of fur.

crystal (quartz)	**kristall** krihs·_tall_	
diamond	**diamant** dee·a·_mant_	
white/yellow gold	**vitt/rött guld** viht/rurtt geuld	
pearl	**pärla** _pair_·la	
I'd like…	**Jag skulle vilja ha…** yahg _skuh_·ler _vihl_·ya hah…	
pewter	**tenn** teen	
platinum	**platina** plah·_tee_·na	
sterling silver	**äkta silver** _ehk_·ta sihl·vehr	
Is this real?	**Är den här äkta?** air dehn hair _ehk_·ta	
Can you engrave it?	**Kan ni gravera den?** kan nee gra·_vee_·ra dehn	

Sport & Leisure

ESSENTIAL

When's the game?	**När börjar matchen?** nair _bur_·yar _ma_·shchehn
Where's…?	**Var ligger…?** vahr _lih_·gehr…
the beach	**stranden** _stran_·dehn
Where's…?	**Var ligger…?** vahr _lih_·gehr…
the park	**parken** _park_·ehn
the pool	**simbassängen** _sihm_·ba·sehng·ehn
Is it safe to swim/ dive here?	**Kan man simma/dyka här utan risk?** kan man _sihmm_·a/_dew_·ka hair _eu_·tan rihsk
Can I rent [hire] golf clubs?	**Kan man hyra golfklubbor?** kan man _hew_·ra _gohlf_·kluh·bohr
How much per hour?	**Vad kostar det per timme?** vahd _kos_·tar dee pair _tihm_·er
How far is it to…?	**Hur långt är det till…?** heur _loangt_ air dee tihl…
Can you show me on the map?	**Kan du visa mig på kartan?** kan deu _vee_ sa may poa _kahr_·tan

Sports and recreation are popular, and there are excellent sports facilities everywhere, ranging from **golf** (golf), **fiske** (fishing), **tennis** (tennis) and **fotboll** (soccer) to **skidåkning** (skiing) and **ishockey** (ice hockey). Tourist offices should have contact information for the various sports facilities in your area. Swedes also love the great outdoors, and the country has much to offer when it comes to **bergklättring** (mountain climbing), **vandring** (hiking), **ridsport** (horsebackriding), **cykelåkning** (cycling), **paddla kanot** (canoeing) and **segling** (boating). Whether you are looking for a day hike or planning a longer trip, some great choices include **Kebnekaise**, which is Sweden's highest mountain, **Kungsleden**, **Bohusleden** or **Padjelantleden**. There are a lot of options for cyclists, both amateurs and professionals, and popular cycle routes include **Kustlinjen** and **Sverigeleden**.

Watching Sport

When's…?	**När börjar…?**	*nair <u>bur</u>•yar…*
the baseball game	**basebollmatchen**	*base•bohl•mat•shehn*
the basketball game	**basketbollmatchen**	*<u>bahs</u>•keht•bohl•ma•shchehn*
the boxing match	**boxningsmatchen**	*boax•nihngs•matsh•ehn*
the cricket game	**cricketspelet**	*cricket•matsh•ehn*
the cycling race	**cykeltävlingen**	*<u>sew</u>•kehl•<u>taiv</u>•lihng•ehn*
the golf tournament	**golfspelet**	*golf•<u>spee</u>•leht*
the soccer [football] game	**fotbollsmatchen**	*<u>foat</u>•bohls•ma•shchehn*
the tennis match	**tennismatchen**	*<u>tehn</u>•ihs•ma•shchehn*
the volleyball game	**volleybollspelet**	*voh•lee•bohl•<u>spee</u>•leht*

Which teams are playing?	**Vilka lag spelar?** <u>vihl</u>•ka lahg <u>spee</u>•lar
Where's the stadium?	**Var ligger idrottsarenan?** vahr <u>lih</u>•gehr <u>ee</u>•drohts•a•<u>ree</u>•nan
Where's the horsetrack/racetrack?	**Var finns hästkapplöpnings/kapplöpningsbanan?** Vahr fihns hehst•kap•luhp•nihngs/kahp•luhp•nihgs•bahn•an
Where can I place a bet?	**Var kan jag spela lotto?** vahr kan yahg <u>spee</u>•la <u>loh</u>•toa

Playing Sport

Is there...nearby?	**Finns det...i närheten?** fihns dee... ee <u>nair</u>•h•ee•ten
a golf course	**en golfbana** ehn <u>gohlf</u>•bah•na
a gym	**ett gym** eht yim
a park	**en park** ehn park
a tennis court	**en tennisbana** ehn <u>tehn</u>•ihs•bah•nohr
How much per...?	**Hur mycket kostar det per...?** heur <u>mew</u>•ker <u>kos</u>•tar dee pair...
day	**dag** dahg
hour	**timme** <u>tihm</u>•er
game	**spel** speel
round	**runda** <u>ruhn</u>•da

Can I rent [hire]...?	**Kan man hyra...?** kan man <u>hew</u>•ra...
golf clubs	**klubbor** <u>kluhb</u>•ohr
equipment	**utrustning** <u>eut</u>•ruhst•nihng
a racket	**en racket** ehn <u>ra</u>•keht

At the Beach/Pool

Where's the beach/pool?	**Var är stranden/simbassängen?** vahr air <u>stran</u>•dehn/<u>sihm</u>•ba•<u>sehng</u>•ehn
Is there a...here?	**Finns det...här?** fihns dee...hair
a kiddie [paddling] pool	**en barnbassäng** ehn <u>bahrn</u>•bah•<u>sehng</u>
an indoor/outdoor pool	**en inomhuspool/utomhuspool** ehn <u>in</u>•ohm•heus•poal/<u>eut</u>•ohm•heus•poal
a lifeguard	**en livräddare** <u>leev</u>•rehd•a•rer
Is it safe to swim/dive?	**Kan man simma/dyka här utan risk?** Kan man <u>sihm</u>•a/<u>dew</u>•ka hair <u>eu</u>•tan rihsk
Is it safe for children?	**Är det barnsäkert?** air dee <u>bahrn</u>•sair•kert
I want to hire...	**Jag skulle vilja hyra...** yahg <u>skuh</u>•ker <u>vihl</u>•ya <u>hew</u>•ra...
a deck chair	**en solstol** ehn <u>soal</u>•stoal
diving equipment	**dykutrustning** dewk•uht•ruhst•a•nihng

147

A significant portion of the Swedish coastline is rough, covered with granite rocks and cliffs and dotted with beaches. Most of the sandy beaches are found in the south and on the southwest coasts. Around Stockholm you can swim and dive from the small islands in the archipelago — and you can even swim in the water around Stockholm itself. Inland lakes, coastal areas and the popular archipelagos of Stockholm and the West Coast are perfect for boaters, and canoeists and kayakers alike.

a jet ski	**en jetski** ehn _jeht_•skee
a motorboat	**en motorbåt** ehn _moa_•tor•b**oat**
a rowboat	**en roddbåt** ehn _rohd_•b**oat**
snorkeling equipment	**snorklingsutrustning** snoh•rklihngs•uht•ruhst•nihng
a surfboard	**en surfbräda** ehn _suhrf_•brair•da
a towel	**en handduk** ehn _hand_•d**euk**
an umbrella	**en solparasol** ehn _soal_•pa•ra•_sohl_
water skis	**vattenskidor** _va_•tehrn•shee•dohr
a windsurfer	**en vindsurfare** ehn vihnd•suhr•fa•reh

For Traveling with Children, see page 157.

Winter Sports

A lift pass for a day/ five days, please.	**Ett liftpass för en dag/för fem dagar, tack.** eht _lihft_•pas furr ehn dahg/furr fehm _dahg_•ar tak
Where's the ice rink?	**Var ligger isbanan?** vahr lee•gehr ihs•b**ahn**•an
Are there lessons?	**Kan man få lektioner?** kan man f**oa** lehk•_shoa_•nehr

---

Swedes grow up with skiing: cross-country in the south and downhill in the north. There are many excellent ski resorts in the north, offering superb skiing and first-class facilities. Many hotels offer three- to seven-day package deals, including transportation and accommodation. In June, try **Riksgränsen** for a taste of skiing in the midnight sun.

Långfärdsbussar (long-distance buses) are efficient, relatively cheap and run daily to all major towns and resorts. Most of the major ski resorts also offer other winter sport activities like snowmobile safaris, snowshoeing and dog sledding tours. **Ishotellet** (Ice Hotel), though not a ski resort specifically, does offer several of these activities.

YOU MAY SEE...

DRAGLIFT	drag lift
ÄGGLIFT	cable car
STOLLIFT	chair lift
NYBÖRJARE	novice
MELLANNIVÅ	intermediate
AVANCERAD	expert
SPÅRET STÄNGD	trail [piste] closed

How much?	**Hur mycket?** *huhr mew•keh*
I'm a beginner.	**Jag är nybörjare.** *yahg air new•bur•yah•reh*
I'm experienced.	**Jag har erfarenhet.** *yahg hahr air•fah•rehn•heet*
I'd like to hire...	**Jag skulle vilja hyra...** *yahg skuh•ler vihl•ya hew•ra...*
boots	**skidpjäxor** *sheed•pyeaix•ohr*
a helmet	**en hjälm** *ehn yehlm*
ice skates	**skridskor** *skrih•skohr*
poles	**stavar** *stah•var*
skis	**skidor** *shee•dohr*
a snowboard	**en snowboard** *ehn snow•board*
snowshoes	**pjäxor** *pyaix•ohr*
These are too big/small.	**De här är för stora/små.** *dehm hair air furr stoa•ra/smoa*
A trail [piste] map, please.	**En karta över spåren, tack.** *ehn kahr•ta ur•vehr spoa•rehn tak*

Out in the Country

I'd like a map of...	**Jag skulle vilja ha en karta över...** *yahg skuh•ler vihl•ya hah ehn kahr•ta ur•vehr...*
this region	**denna region** *dehn•a reh•gioan*

walking routes	**vandringsleder**	_van_·drihngs·_lee_·dehr
cycle routes	**cykeleder**	_sew_·kehl·_lee_·dehr
the trails	**spåren**	_spoa_·rehn
Is it easy/difficult?	**Är det lätt/svårt?**	air dee leht/svoart
Is it far/steep?	**Är det långt/brant?**	air dee loangt/brant
How far is it to…?	**Hur långt är det till…?**	heur _loangt_ air dee tihl…
Can you show me on the map?	**Kan du visa mig på kartan?**	kan deu _vee_·sa may poa _kahr_·tan
I'm lost.	**Jag har kommit vilse.**	yahg hahr _koh_·miht _vihl_·ser
Where's…?	**Var ligger…?**	vahr _lih_·gehr…
the bridge	**bron**	_broan_
the cave	**grottan**	_groht_·an
the cliff	**klippa**	_klihp_·an
the farm	**bondgården**	_boand_·_goa_rd·ehn
the field	**åkern**	_oak_·ern
the footpath	**fotvandringsleden**	_foat_·vand·rihngs·_lee_·dehn
the forest	**skogen**	_skoag_·ehn
the hill	**berget**	_behr_·yeht
the lake	**sjön**	_shurn_
the mountain	**berget**	_behr_·yeht
the mountain pass	**bergspasset**	_berys_·pas·eht
the mountain range	**bergskedjan**	_berys_·chee·dyan
the nature reserve	**naturreservatet**	na·_teur_·res·her·_vah_·teht
the panorama	**panoraman**	pan·o·_rah_·man
the park	**parken**	_park_·ehn
the path	**stigen**	stee·gehn
Where's…?	**Var ligger…?**	vahr _lih_·gehr…
the peak	**toppen**	_tohp_·ehn
the picnic area/ rest area	**picknickområdet/rastplatsen**	pihk·nihk·ohm·_roa_·det/_rast_·plats·ehn

the pond	**dammen** *dah·mehn*
the river	**floden** *<u>fload</u>·ehn*
the sea	**havet** *<u>hafv</u>·eht*
the hot spring	**den varma källan** *dehn var·ma cheh·lan*
the valley	**dalen** *<u>dahl</u>·ehn*
the viewpoint	**utsiktspunkten** *<u>eut</u>·sihkts·peunk·tehn*
the village	**byn** *bewn*
the vineyard	**vinodlingen** *vihn·ohd·lihng·ehn*
the waterfall	**vattenfallet** *<u>va</u>·tehrn·fal*

Going Out

ESSENTIAL

Do you have a program of events?	**Har ni ett evenemangsprogram?** *hahr nee eht eh·vehn·eh·<u>mangs</u>·proa·gram*
What's playing at the movies [cinema] tonight?	**Vad visas på bio ikväll?** *vahd <u>vee</u>·sas poa <u>bee</u>·oa ee·<u>kvehl</u>*
Where's...?	**Var ligger...?** *vahr <u>lih</u>·gehr...*
the downtown area	**centrum** *<u>sehn</u>·truhm*
the bar	**baren** *<u>bah</u>·rehn*
the dance club	**diskoteket** *dis·koh·<u>tee</u>·keht*

Entertainment

Can you recommend...?	**Kan du rekommendera...?** *kan deu reh·koh·mehn·<u>dee</u>·ra...*
a concert	**en konsert** *ehn kohn·<u>sair</u>*
a movie	**en film** *ehn film*

an opera	**en opera** ehn _oa_·peh·ra
a play	**en teaterpjäs** ehn tee·_ah_·tehr·pjais
When does it start/end?	**När börjar/slutar den?** nair _bur_·yar/_sleu_·tar dehn
What's the dress code?	**Vilken klädsel gäller?** _vihl_·kehn klaid·sehl _gehl_·lehr
I like…	**Jag tycker om…** yahg _tew_·kehr ohm…
classical music	**klassisk musik** _klas_·isk meu·_seek_
folk music	**folkmusik** _folk_·meu·_seek_
jazz	**jazz** yas
pop music	**popmusik** _pop_·meu·_seek_
rap	**rap** rap

For Tickets, see page 21.

YOU MAY HEAR…

Stäng av mobiltelefonen, tack. stehng afv mo·_beel_·teh·leh·_foa_·nen tak

Turn off your cell [mobile] phones, please.

Nightlife

What's there to do at night?	**Vad kan man göra på kvällarna?** vahd kan man _yur_·ra poa _kvehl_·ar·na
Can you recommend…?	**Kan du rekommendera…?** kan deu reh·koh·mehn·_dee_·ra…
a bar	**en bar** ehn bahr
a casino	**ett kasino** eht ka·_see_·noh
a dance club	**ett diskotek** eht dis·koh·_tehk_
a gay club	**en gayklubb** ehn _gay_·kluhb
a jazz club	**en jazzklubb** ehn _yas_·kluhb

a club with local music	**en klubb med lokal musik** *ehn kluhb meed lo-kahl meu-seek*
a nightclub	**en nattklubb** *ehn nat-kluhb*
Is there live music?	**Spelar man livemusik där?** *spee-lar man live-meu-seek dair*
How do I get there?	**Hur kan jag komma dit?** *heur kan yahg koh-ma deet*
Is there a cover charge?	**Är det kuvertavgift?** *air de keu-vair-afv-yihft*
Let's go dancing.	**Vi går ut och dansar.** *vee goar eut ohk dan-sar*
Is this area safe at night?	**Är detta område säkert på natten?** *ehr deh-ta ohm-roh-deh seh-kehrt poh na-tehn*

153

Sweden has produced several world famous pop and rock bands, and music is an important part of contemporary culture and entertainment. The government generously supports independent musicians, as well as smaller music groups, orchestras and symphonies. In larger cities and towns you'll easily find concerts and performances to attend, and information should be listed at the tourist office or its webpage regarding upcoming concerts and events. If you are traveling in Sweden during the summer, attending a music festival is an unforgettable experience. **The Peace & Love Festival** in Borlänge, just two hours from Stockholm, is popular among the younger crowd. Stockholm is home to **Ung08**, which is Europe's largest youth festival, geared toward 13-19 year olds. **The Hultsfred Festival**, in southern Sweden, is the oldest and largest festival. There are also a host of other music festivals covering everything from folk music, to pop and jazz.

Special Requirements

Business Travel   155
Traveling with Children 157
Disabled Travelers   160

Business Travel

ESSENTIAL

I'm here on business.	**Jag är här på affärsresa.**	*yahg air hair poa a·fairs·ree·sa*
Here's my business card.	**Här är mitt kort.**	*hair air miht koart*
Can I have your card?	**Kan jag få ditt kort?**	*kan yahg foa diht koart*
I have a meeting with...	**Jag har ett möte med...**	*yahg hahr eht mur·ter meed...*
Where's...?	**Var ligger...?**	*vahr lih·gehr...*
the business center	**businesscentret**	*bihs·nihs·sehn·treht*
the convention hall	**kongresshallen**	*kohn·grehs·ha·lehn*
the meeting room	**konferensrummet**	*kohn·feh·rans·ruhm·eht*

On Business

I'm here to attend...	**Jag är här för att delta i...**	*yahg air hair furr at deel·tah ee...*
a seminar	**ett seminarium**	*eht sehm·i·nah·ree·uhm*
a conference	**en konferens**	*ehn kohn·fehr·ans*
a meeting	**ett sammanträde**	*eht sam·an·trai·der*
My name is...	**Jag heter...**	*yahg hee·ter...*
May I introduce my colleague...	**Får jag presentera min kollega...**	*foar yahg prehs·ehn·tee·ra mihn koh·lee·ga...*
Nice to meet you.	**Trevligt att träffas.**	*treev·ligt at trehf·as*
I have a meeting/an appointment with...	**Jag har ett möte/en träff med...**	*yahg hahr eht mut·eh/ehn trehf·mehd*
I'm sorry I'm late.	**Ursäkta för att jag är sen.**	*eur·shehk·ta furr at yahg air sehn*

I'd like an interpreter.	**Jag behöver en tolk.** *yahg beh•hur•ver ehn tohlk*
You can reach me at the…Hotel.	**Du kan nå mig på hotell…** *deu kan noa may poa ho•tehl…*
I'm here until…	**Jag stannar till…** *yahg stan•ar tihl…*
I need to…	**Jag behöver…** *yahg beh•hur•ver…*
make a call	**ringa ett samtal** *rihng•a eht sam•tahl*
make a photocopy	**göra en kopia** *gur•ra ehn koh•pee•ya*

YOU MAY HEAR…

Har ni bokat tid? *hahr nee boa•kat teed*	Do you have an appointment?
Med vem? *meed vehm*	With whom?
Han/Hon sitter i möte. *han/hoan sih•ter ee mur•ter*	He/She is in a meeting.
Ett ögonblick, tack. *eht ur•gohn•blik tak*	One moment, please.
Varsågod och sitt. *Vahr•soa•gohd ohk siht*	Have a seat.
Vill du ha något att dricka? *Vihl deu hah nohgoht at drih•ka*	Would you like something to drink?
Tack för att ni kom. *tak furr at nee kom*	Thank you for coming.

send an e-mail	**skicka e-post** _shihk·a ee·pohst_
send a fax	**skicka en fax** _shihk·a ehn fax_
send a package (overnight)	**skicka ett paket (med expressutdelning)** _shihk·a eht pa·keet (meed ehx·prehs·eut·deel·nihng)_

For Communications, see page 49.

Traveling with Children

ESSENTIAL

Is there a discount for kids?	**Har ni barnrabatt?** _hahr nee bahrn·rah·bat_
Can you recommend a babysitter?	**Kan du rekommendera en barnvakt?** _kan deu reh·koh·mehn·dee·ra ehn bahrn·vakt_
Could I have a highchair?	**Kan jag få en barnstol, tack?** _kan yahg foa ehn bahrn·stoal tak_
Where can I change the baby?	**Var kan jag byta på babyn?** _vahr kan yahg bew·ta poa bai·been_
Where's…?	**Var ligger…?** _vahr lih·gehr…_
the amusement park	**nöjesfältet** _nury·ehs·fehl·teht_
the arcade	**arkadhallen** _ar·kahd·ha·lehn_
the kiddie [paddling] pool	**barnbassängen** _bahrn·ba·sehng·ehn_
the park	**parken** _park·kehn_
the playground	**lekplatsen** _leek·plats·ehn_
the zoo	**djurparken** _yeur·park·ehn_
Are kids allowed?	**Får man ta barnen med?** _foar man tah bahr·nehn meed_
Is it safe for kids?	**Är det barnsäkert?** _air det bahrn·sair·kert_

YOU MAY HEAR...

Vad gullig! vahd <u>geul</u>•ig

Vad heter han/hon? vahd <u>hee</u>•tehr han/hoan

Hur gammal är han/hon? heur <u>gam</u>•al air han/hoan

How cute!

What's his/her name?

How old is he/she?

Out & About

Can you recommend something for kids?	**Kan du föreslå något för barn?** kan deu furr•reh•sloa <u>noa</u>•goht furr bahrn
Where's…?	**Var är…?** Vahr air…
the amusement park	**nöjesparken** nuy•ehs•pahr•kehn
the arcade	**gallerian** gah•le•ree•an
the kiddie [paddling] pool	**barnbassängen/plaskdammen** bah•rn•ba•sehng•ehn/plask•da•mehn
the park	**parken** par•kehn
the playground	**lekplatsen** lehk•plat•sehn
the zoo	**djurparken** yeur•par•kehn
Are kids allowed?	**Tillåts barn?** tihl•oats bahrn
Is it safe for kids?	**Är det säkert för barn?** air deht seh•kehrt furr bahrn
Is it suitable for…year olds?	**Passar det för…-åringar?** <u>pas</u>•ar dee furr…<u>oa</u>•rihng•ar

For Numbers, see page 179.

Baby Essentials

Do you have…?	**Har ni…?** *hahr nee…*	
a baby bottle	**en nappflaska** *ehn nap·flas·ka*	
baby food	**babymat** *behy·bih·maht*	
baby wipes	**våtservetter för barn** *voat·ser·veht·er fur·rbahrn*	
a car seat	**en bilbarnstol** *ehn beel·bahrn·stoal*	
a children's menu	**en barnmeny** *ehn bahrn·meh·new*	
a children's portion	**en barnportion** *bahrn·pohrt·shoan*	
a highchair	**en barnstol** *ehn bahrn·stoal*	
a crib	**en barnsäng** *ehn bahrn·sehng*	
diapers [nappies]	**blöjor** *blury·ohr*	
formula	**välling** *vehl·ihng*	
a pacifier [dummy]	**en napp** *ehn nap*	
a playpen	**ett lekrum** *eht leek·ruhm*	
a stroller [pushchair]	**en sittvagn** *ehn siht·vangn*	
Can I breastfeed the baby here?	**Får jag amma barnet här?** *foar yahg ah·ma bahr·neht hair*	
Where can I change the baby?	**Var kan jag byta på babyn?** *vahr kan yahg bew·ta poa bai·been*	

For Dining with Children, see page 64.

Babysitting

Can you recommend a reliable babysitter?	**Kan du rekommendera en pålitlig barnvakt?** *kaun deu re·koh·mehn·dee·rahra ehn poa·leet·lihg bahrn·vakt*
What's the charge?	**Vad kostar det?** *vahd kos·tar dee*
We'll be back by…	**Vi kommer tillbaka** *Vee koh·mehr tihl·bah·ka*
I'll pick them up at…	**Jag hämtar dem…** *yahg hehm·tar dehm…*
I can be reached at…	**Du kan nå mig på…** *deu kan noa may poa…*

For Time, see page 181.

Health & Emergency

Can you recommend a pediatrician?	**Kan du rekommendera en barnläkare?** *kan deu reh•koh•men•dee•ra ehn bahrn•lairk•a•rer*
My child is allergic to...	**Mitt barn är allergiskt mot...** *miht bahrn air a•lehr•gisk moat...*
My child is missing.	**Mitt barn har kommit bort.** *miht bahrn hahr koh•miht bohrt*
Have you seen a boy/girl?	**Har du sett en pojke/flicka?** *hahr deu seht ehn poy•ker/flih•ka*

For Meals & Cooking, see page 65.

For Health, see page 166.

For Police, see page 164.

Disabled Travelers

ESSENTIAL

Is there...?	**Finns det...?** *fihns det...*
access for the disabled	**ingång för rörelsehindrade** *in•goang furr rur•rehl•seh•hihn•dra•der*
a wheelchair ramp	**en rullstolsramp** *ehn reul•stoals•ramp*
a handicapped-[disabled-] accessible toilet	**en handikappanpassad toalett** *ehn hand•ee•kap•an•pas•ad toa•ah•leht*
I need...	**Jag behöver...** *yahg beh•hur•ver...*
assistance	**hjälp** *yehlp*
an elevator [lift]	**en hiss** *ehn hihs*
a ground floor room	**ett rum på bottenvåningen** *eht ruhm poa boh•tehrn•voa•nihng•hen*

Asking for Assistance

I'm disabled.	**Jag är handikappad.** *yahg air <u>hand</u>•ee•kap•ad*
I'm deaf.	**Jag är döv.** *yahg air durv*
I'm visually/hearing impaired.	**Jag är synskadad/hörselskadad.** *yahg air <u>sewn</u>•skah•dad/hur•sel•<u>skah</u>•dad*
I'm unable to walk far/use the stairs.	**Jag kan inte gå långt/gå i trappor.** *yahg kan <u>ihn</u>•ter goa loangt/goa ee <u>trap</u>•ohr*
Can I bring my wheelchair?	**Kan jag ta med min rullstol?** *kan yahg tah meed mihn <u>ruhl</u>•stoal*
Are guide dogs permitted?	**Är det tillåtet med ledarhund?** *air dee tihl•<u>loa</u>•teht meed <u>leed</u>•ar•huhnd*
Can you help me?	**Kan du hjälpa mig?** *kan deu yehl•pa may*
Could you open/hold the door?	**Kan du öppna/hålla upp dörren?** *kan deu <u>urp</u>•na/ <u>hoa</u>•la uhp <u>dur</u>•rehn*

In an Emergency

Emergencies	163
Police	164
Health	166
The Basics	175

Emergencies

ESSENTIAL

Help!	**Hjälp!** *yelp*
Go away!	**Ge er iväg!** *yeh ehr ee•vairg*
Stop thief!	**Stoppa tjuven!** *stop•a shcheu•vehn*
Get a doctor!	**Hämta en läkare!** *hehm•ta ehn lair•ka•rer*
Fire!	**Det brinner!** *dee brihn•ehr*
I'm lost.	**Jag har gått vilse.** *yahg hahr goat vihl•ser*
Can you help me?	**Kan du hjälpa mig?** *kan deu yehl•pa may*

YOU MAY HEAR...

Fyll i blanketten, tack. *fewl ee blan•keht•ehn tak*
Please fill out this form.

Er legitimation, tack. *ehr lehg•ee•tih•ma•shoan tak*
Your identification, please.

När/Var hände det? *nair/vahr hehn•dehr dee*
When/Where did it happen?

Hur ser han/hon ut? *hewr seer han/hoan eut*
What does he/she look like?

Police

ESSENTIAL

Call the police!	**Ring polisen!** *rihng poa·lee·sehn*
Where's the nearest police station?	**Var ligger närmaste polisstation?** *vahr lih·gehr nair·mas·ter poo·lees·sta·shoan*
There's been an accident.	**Det har hänt en olycka.** *det hahr hehnt ehn oa·lewk·a*
I've been attacked.	**Jag har blivit anfallen.** *jahg hahr blee·viht an·fa·lehn*
My child is missing.	**Mitt barn har kommit bort.** *miht bahrn hahr koh·miht bohrt*
I need...	**Jag behöver...** *yahg beh·hur·vehr...*
an interpreter	**en tolk** *ehn tohlk*
to contact my lawyer	**kontakta min advokat** *kohn·tak·ta mihn ad·voh·kaht*
to make a phone call	**ringa ett samtal** *rihng·a eht sam·tahl*
I'm innocent.	**Jag är oskyldig.** *yahg air oa·shewl·dihg*

Crime & Lost Property

I want to report...	**Jag vill anmäla...** *yahg vihl an·mair·la...*
a mugging	**ett överfall** *eht ur·vehr·fal*
a rape	**en våldtäkt** *ehn vohld·tehkt*
a theft	**ett rån** *eht roan*
I've been robbed/mugged.	**Jag har blivit rånad/överfallen.** *yahg hahr blee·viht roa·nad/ur·veh·fal·ehn*
I've lost...	**Jag har tappet...** *yahg hahr tah·pat...*

My...has been stolen.	**Någon har stulit...** <u>noa</u>·gohn hahr <u>steu</u>·liht...
backpack	**min ryggsäck** mihn <u>rewg</u>·sehk
bicycle	**min cykel** mihn <u>sew</u>·kehl
camera	**min kamera** mihn <u>kah</u>·meh·ra
rental car	**min bil/hyrbil** mihn beel/<u>hewr</u>·beel
computer	**min dator** mihn <u>dah</u>·tohr
credit cards	**mina kreditkort** mee·na kre·<u>deet</u>·koart
jewelry	**mina smycken** mee·na <u>smew</u>·ken
money	**mina pengar** mee·na <u>pehng</u>·ar
passport	**mitt pass** miht pas
purse [handbag]	**min portmonnä** mihn pohrt·mo·<u>nai</u>
traveler's checks [cheques]	**mina resecheckar** <u>mee</u>·na <u>ree</u>·seh·shehk·ar
wallet	**min plånbok** mihn <u>ploan</u>·boak
I need a police report for my insurance.	**Jag behöver en polisanmälan till min försäkring.** yahg beh·hu·vehr ehn poal·ees·an·mailan tihl meen furr·sehk·rihng
Where is the British/American/Irish embassy?	**Var ligger den brittiska/amerikanska ambassaden?** var ligger den brittiska/amerikanska ambassaden?

Health

ESSENTIAL

I'm sick [ill].	**Jag är sjuk.** *yahg air sheuk*
I need an English-speaking doctor.	**Jag behöver en engelsktalande läkare.** *yahg beh•hur•vehr ehn ehng•ehlsk•tahl•an•der lair•ka•rer*
It hurts here.	**Det gör ont här.** *dee yurr oant hair*
I have a stomachache.	**Jag har ont i magen.** *yahg hahr oant ee mah•gehn*

Finding a Doctor

Can you recommend a doctor/dentist?	**Kan du rekommendera en läkare/tandläkare?** *kan deu reh•koh•mehn•dee•ra ehn lair•ka•rer/ tand•lair•ka•rer*
Can the doctor come to see me here?	**Kan doktorn komma och undersöka mig här?** *kan dohk•torn koh•ma ohk eun•der•sur•ka may hair*
I need an English-speaking doctor.	**Jag behöver en engelsktalande läkare.** *yahg beh•uv•ehr en eeng•ehlsk•tah•lan•de leh•ka•re*
What are their office hours?	**Vilka är deras öppettider?** *vihl•ka air dee•ras ur•peh•tee•dehr*
Can I make an appointment for...?	**Kan jag boka en tid...?** *kan yahg boa•ka ehn teed...*
today	**idag** *ee•dahg*
tomorrow	**imorgon** *ee•mo•ron*
as soon as possible	**så snart som möjligt** *soa snahrt som mury•ligt*
It's urgent.	**Det är brådskande.** *dee air broas•kan•der*

Symptoms

I'm...	**Jag...** *yahg...*
bleeding	**blöder** _blur_·dehr
constipated	**är förstoppad** air furr·_stop_·ad
dizzy	**har yrsel** hahr _ewr_·sehl
nauseous	**mår illa**. moar _ihl_·la
vomiting	**kräks**. krairks
It hurts here.	**Det gör ont här.** dee yurr oant hair
I have...	**Jag har...** yahg hahr...
an allergic reaction	**en allergisk reaktion** ehn a·lehr·_gihsk_ ree·ak·_shoan_
chest pain	**ont i bröstet** oant ee _brurs_·teht
cramps	**kramper** kram·pehr
diarrhea	**diarré** dee·ar·ee
an earache	**ont i örat** oant ee _ur_·rat
a fever	**feber** _fee_·behr
pain	**ont** oant
a rash	**ett utslag** eht _eut_·slahg
a sprain	**en stukning** ehn _steuk_·nihng
some swelling	**en lätt svullnad** ehn leht _sveul_·nad
a stomachache	**ont i magen** oant ee _mah_·gehn
sunstroke	**solsting** _soal_·stihng
I've been sick [ill] for...days.	**Jag har varit sjuk i...dagar.** yahg hahr _vah_·riht sheuk ee..._dah_·gar

For Numbers, see page 179.

Conditions

I'm anemic/diabetic.	**Jag är anemisk/diabetiker.** yahg air a·_nee_·mihsk/ dee·a·_beh_·tih·ker
I'm epileptic.	**Jag har epilepsi** yahg hahr eh·pih·leh·psi
I'm allergic to antibiotics/penicillin.	**Jag är allergisk mot antibiotika/penicillin.** yahg air a·lehr·_gihsk_ moat an·tih·bee·_oa_·tee·ka/pehn·eh·si·_leen_

YOU MAY HEAR...

Vad är det för fel? *vahd air dee fur feel*
What's wrong?

Var gör det ont? *vahr yur dee oant*
Where does it hurt?

Gör det ont här? *yur deht ohnt hehr*
Does it hurt here?

Tar du någon annan medicin? *tahr deu noa•gohn an•an meh•dih•seen*
Are you taking any other medication?

Är du allergisk mot något? *air deu a•lehr•gihsk moat noa•goht*
Are you allergic to anything?

Öppna munnen. *urp•na muhn•ehn*
Open your mouth.

Andas djupt. *an•das yeupt*
Breathe deeply.

Hosta, tack. *hoas•ta, tak*
Cough, please.

Du behöver åka till sjukhuset. *deu beh•hur•vehr oa•ka tihl sjeuk•heu•seht*
You need to go to the hospital.

I have...	**Jag har...** *yahg hahr...*
arthritis	**artrit** *ar•treet*
asthma	**astma** *as•ma*
high/low blood pressure	**högt/låg blodtryck** *hurgt/loagt blood•trewk*
a heart condition	**hjärtproblem** *yairt•proa•bleem*
I'm taking... (medicine).	**Jag tar...(medicin).** *yahg tahr...* *(meh•dee•seen)*

Treatment

| Can you prescribe a generic drug [unbranded medication]? | **Kan du skriva ut ett generiskt läkemedel [generika]?** *Kahn deu skrih•va eut eht gehn•eh•rih•skt lai•keh•meh•dehl [gehn•eh•rih•ka]* |
| Where can I get it? | **Var hittar jag det?** *vahr hih•tar yahg deht* |

Do I need a prescription/ medicine?	**Behöver jag ett recept/medicin?** *beh·hur·vehr yahg eht reh·sehpt/meh·dih·sihn*

For Pharmacy, see page 171.

Hospital

Please notify my family.	**Var snäll och underrätta min familj.** *vahr snehl ohk eun·der·rehta mihn fa·mily*
I'm in pain.	**Jag har ont.** *yahg hahr oant*
I need a doctor/nurse.	**Jag behöver en läkare/sjuksköterska.** *yahg beh·hur·vehr ehn lair·ka·rer/sheuk·shur·ter·ska*
When are visiting hours?	**När är det besökstid?** *nair air dee beh·surks·teed*
I'm visiting...	**Jag vill besöka...** *yahg vihl beh·sur·ka...*

Dentist

I've broken a tooth/lost a filling.	**Jag har brutit av en tand/tappat en plomb.** *yahg hahr breu·tiht afv ehn tand/tap·at ehn plohmb*
This tooth hurts.	**Den här tanden gör ont.** *dehn hair tan·dehn yur oant*
Can you fix this denture?	**Kan du reparera den här tandprotesen?** *kan deu reh·pa·ree·ra dehn hair tand·proh·tees·ehn*

Gynecologist

I have menstrual cramps/a vaginal infection.	**Jag har mens värk/en vaginal infektion.** *yahg hahr mens vehrk/ehn va·gih·nahl ihn·fehk·shoan*
I missed my period.	**Min mens har inte kommit.** *mihn mehns hahr ihn·ter koh·miht*
I'm on the Pill.	**Jag tar p-piller.** *yahg tahr pee·pihl·ler*
I'm (...months) pregnant.	**Jag är (...månader) gravid.** *Yahg air (...moh·na·dehr) gra·veed*
I'm (not) pregnant.	**Jag är (inte) gravid.** *yahg air (ihn·ter) gra·veed*

| I haven't had my period for…months. | **Jag har inte haft mens på… månader.** *yahg hahr ihn•ter haft mehns poa… moa•na•dehr* |

For Numbers, see page 179.

Optician

I've lost…	**Jag har tappat…** *yahg hahr tap•at…*
a contact lens	**en kontaktlins** *ehn kohn•takt•lihns*
my glasses	**mina glasögon** *mee•na glahs•ur•gohn*
a lens	**en lins** *ehn lihns*

Payment & Insurance

How much does it cost?	**Hur mycket kostar det?** *heur mew•ker kos•tar dee*
Can I pay by credit card?	**Kan jag betala med kreditkort?** *kan yahg beh•tah•la meed kreh•deet•koart*
I have insurance.	**Jag har försäkring.** *yahg hahr furr•sair•krihng*
Can I have a receipt for my insurance?	**Kan jag få ett kvitto för mitt försäkringsbolag?** *kan yahg foa eht kvih•toh furr miht furr•sair•krihngs•boa•lahg*

Pharmacy

ESSENTIAL

Where's the nearest pharmacy?	**Var är närmaste apotek?** *vahr air nair•mas•teh a•poa•teek*
What time does the pharmacy open/close?	**När öppnar/stänger apoteket?** *nair urp•nar/ stehng•ehr a•poa•tee•keht*
What would you recommend for...?	**Vad kan du rekommendera för...?** *vahd kan deu reh•koh•mehn•dee•ra furr...*
How much should I take?	**Hur mycket ska jag ta?** *heur mew•ker skah yahg tah*
Can you fill [make up] this prescription for me?	**Kan ni göra iordning det här receptet åt mig?** *kan nee yur•ra ee oard•nihng dee hair reh•sehp•teht oat may*
I'm allergic to...	**Jag är allergisk mot...** *yahg air a•lehr•gihsk moat...*

In addition to filling prescriptions, **apotek** (pharmacies) sell over-the-counter medication as well as their own brands of toiletries and cosmetics. Almost all pharmacies are open on weekdays, but not all are open late in the evening or on weekends. Business hours vary considerably depending on the pharmacy. Generally, business hours are between 9:00 a.m. and 5:00 p.m. on weekdays. Locations with evening hours usually close around 9:00 p.m., and weekend hours are generally 10:00 a.m. to 4:00 p.m.

What to Take

How much should I take?	**Hur mycket ska jag ta?** *heur mew·ker skah yahg tah*
How many times a day should I take it?	**Hur många gånger om dagen ska jag ta det?** *heur moang·a goang·er ohm dah·gehn skah yahg tah dee*
Is it suitable for children?	**Är det lämpligt för barn?** *air dee lehmp·lihgt furr bahrn*
I'm taking...(medicine).	**Jag tar...(medicin).** *yahg tahr... (meh·dee·seen)*
Are there side effects?	**Ger det några biverkningar?** *yehr dee noa·gra bee·vehrk·nihng·ar*
I'd like some medicine for...	**Jag behöver medicin mot...** *yahg beh·hur·vehr meh·dih·seen moat...*
a cold	**en förkylning** *ehn furr·chewl·nihng*
a cough	**hosta** *hoas·ta*
diarrhea	**diarré** *dee·a·reh*
a headache	**huvudvärk** *huh·vuhd·vairk*
an insect bite	**ett insektbett** *eht in·sekt·beht*
motion sickness	**åksjuka** *oak·sheu·ka*

YOU MAY SEE...

EN GÅNG/TRE GÅNGER PER DAG	once/three times a day
TABLETTER	tablets
DROPPAR TESKEDAR	drop teaspoons
FÖRE/EFTER/TILLSAMMANS MED MÅLTIDER	before/after/with meals
PÅ FASTANDE MAGE	on an empty stomach
SVÄLJS HELA	swallow whole
KAN ORSAKA DÅSIGHET	may cause drowsiness
ENDAST FÖR UTVÄRTES BRUK	for external use only

a sore throat	**halsont** <u>hals</u>·oant
a sunburn	**solbränna** <u>soal</u>·brehn·a
a toothache	**tandvärk** tand·vairk
an upset stomach	**ont i magen** oant ee <u>mah</u>·gehn

Basic Supplies

I'd like...	**Jag skulle vilja ha...** yahg <u>skuh</u>·ler <u>vihl</u>·ya hah...
acetaminophen [paracetamol]	**acetominofen** a·seht·a·mihn·oa·<u>fehn</u>
antiseptic cream	**antiseptisk salva** an·tih·<u>sehp</u>·tihsk sal·va
aspirin	**huvudvärkstabletter** heu·vuhd·vairks·ta·<u>bleh</u>·ter
bandage [plasters]	**gasbinda** <u>gahs</u>·bihn·da
a comb	**kam** kam
condoms	**kondomer** kohn·<u>doa</u>·mehr
contact lens solution	**kontaktlinsvätska** kohn·<u>takt</u>·lins·veht·ska
deodorant	**deodorant** dee·oa·deh·<u>rant</u>
a hairbrush	**en hårborste** ehn <u>hoar</u>·bohrsh·ter
hair spray	**hårspray** <u>hoar</u>·spray
ibuprofen	**ibuprofen** ee·beu·proa·<u>fehn</u>
insect repellent	**myggolja** <u>mewg</u>·ohl·ya

a nail file	**en nagelfil**	*ehn nah-gehl-feel*
a (disposable) razor	**en (engångs)-rakhyvel**	*ehn (een-goangs)-rahk-hew-vehl*
razor blades	**rakblad**	*rahk-blahd*
sanitary napkins [towels]	**bindor**	*bin-dohr*
shampoo/	**schampo**	*sham-poa*
conditioner	**hårbalsam**	*hoar-bal-sam*
soap	**tvål**	*tvoal*
sunscreen	**solskyddskräm**	*soal-shewds-krairm*
tampons	**tamponger**	*tam-poang-ehr*
tissue	**papper näsdukar**	*pa-pehrs-nairs-deu-kar*
toilet paper	**toalettpapper**	*toa-a-leht-pa-pehr*
a toothbrush	**tandborste**	*tand-bohr-ster*
toothpaste	**tandkräm**	*tand-krairm*

For Baby Essentials, see page 159.

The Basics

Grammar

Regular Verbs

The present tense of regular verbs in Swedish is formed by adding either -**r** or
-**er** to the stem. If the stem ends in **a**, add an -**r**, if it ends in a consonant add
-**er**. The past tense is formed by adding either -**de** or -**te** to the basic form. If
the basic form ends in a **p**, **t**, **k** or **s**, add -**te**, if not then add -**de**. The future is
formed by adding the present tense of **ska** (will) + the verb in the infinitive.
This applies to all persons (e.g., I, you, he, she, it, etc.). Following are the
present, past and future forms of the verbs **att köpa** (to buy) and **att fråga**
(to ask). The different conjugation endings are in bold.

	Present	Past	Future
att köpa (to buy)	köp**er**	köp**te**	ska köpa
att fråga (to ask)	fråga**r**	fråga**de**	ska fråga

Pronouns

I	**jag**	it (common/neuter)	**den/det**
you (sing.,inf.)	**du**	we	**vi**
he	**han**	you (pl.)	**ni**
she	**hon**	they	**de**

In Swedish there are two terms for 'you': **du** (singular/informal) and **ni**
(plural/informal). Both are used when talking to relatives, friends, colleagues,
children, between young people and in work situations. The plural form, **ni**,
is used in more formal situations to refer to one or more persons. Its use has
however become less frequent, so nowadays you will hear most people address
each other with **du**.

Irregular Verbs

There are a number of irregular verbs in Swedish; these must be memorized. Like regular verbs, however, the irregular verb form remains the same, irrespective of person. The table below shows the present, past and future conjugations for a number of important, useful irregular verbs.

	Present	Past	Future
att vara (to be)	är	var	ska vara
att ha (to have)	har	hade	ska ha
att komma (to come)	kommer	kom	ska komma
att göra (to do)	gör	gjorde	ska göra
att gå (to go/walk)	går	gick	ska gå

sing. = singular, inf. = informal, pl. = plural

Word Order

Swedish is similar to English in terms of word order for simple sentences: It follows the subject-verb-object pattern.

Example:

Sara läser en bok. Sara is reading a book.

When the sentence doesn't begin with a subject, the word order changes; the verb and the subject are inverted.

Example:

Nu läser Sara en bok. Now Sara is reading a book.

However, **nu** could just as well be placed at the end of the sentence, e.g. **Sara läser en bok nu.**

Questions are formed by reversing the order of the subject and verb:

Du ser katten.	You see the cat.
Ser du katten?	Do you see the cat?

Negations

A statement can be negated by inserting the word **inte** after the verb:

Jag talar svenska.   I speak Swedish.
Jag talar inte svenska.   I do not speak Swedish.

Nouns & Articles

The indefinite article (a, an) is expressed with **en** for common nouns and with **ett** for neuter nouns. Generally, common nouns can be both feminine and masculine (e.g. people, animals, etc.); neuter nouns have no gender (e.g. house, roof, etc.). However, there are several exceptions to this rule.

In Swedish, there are five different endings used to form plural nouns; three correspond to common gender nouns and two to neuter gender nouns. The following rules apply to nouns in the indefinite singular.

1. **en** words that end in -**a** take an -**or** ending
2. **en** words that end in -**e** take an -**ar** ending
3. **en** words with stress on the last vowel take an -**er** ending
4. **ett** words that end in a vowel take an -**n** ending
5. **ett** words that end in a consonant take no additional ending

Common gender nouns that end in a consonant are not covered by the rules above. These words will take either an -**ar** ending or an -**er** ending. The nouns which fall into this category will simply need to be memorized.

Singular indefinite	Plural indefinite
en flicka (a girl)	flick*or*
en timme (an hour)	timm*ar*
en telefon (a telephone)	telefon*er*
ett konto (an account)	kont*on*
ett hus (a house)	hus
en bil (a car)	bil*ar*

Definite articles: where in English we say 'the car', the Swedes say the equivalent of 'car-the', i.e. they tag the definite article onto the end of the noun. In the singular, common nouns take an **-en** ending, neuter nouns an **-et** ending. In the plural, common nouns add an **-na** and neuter nouns take an **-en** ending, neuter nouns an **-et** ending. In the plural, common nouns add an **-na** and neuter nouns take an **-en**.

	Singular	Plural
common gender	**katten** the cat	**katterna** the cats
neuter gender	**tåget** the train	**tågen** the trains

Demonstrative Adjectives

	Common	Neuter	Plural
this/these	**denna**	**detta**	**dessa**
that/those	**den**	**det**	**de**
	denna bil	**detta hus**	
	(this car)	(this house)	

Possessive Adjectives

	Common	Neuter	Plural
my	**min**	**mitt**	**mina**
your (sing.)	**din**	**ditt**	**dina**
our	**vår**	**vårt**	**våra**
his	**hans**		
hers		**hennes**	
its		**dess/dess**	
their		**deras**	
your (pl.)	**er**	**ert**	**era**

Adverbs & Adverbial Expressions

Adverbs are generally formed by adding **-t** to the corresponding adjective.

Hon går snabbt. She walks quickly.
Snabb quick

Numbers

ESSENTIAL

0	**noll** *nohl*	
1	**ett** *eht*	
2	**två** *tvoa*	
3	**tre** *tree*	
4	**fyra** *few·ra*	
5	**fem** *fehm*	
6	**sex** *sehx*	
7	**sju** *sheu*	
8	**åtta** *oh·ta*	
9	**nio** *nee·oa*	
10	**tio** *tee·oa*	
11	**elva** *ehl·va*	
12	**tolv** *tohlv*	
13	**tretton** *treh·tohn*	
14	**fjorton** *fyeur·tohn*	
15	**femton** *fehm·tohn*	
16	**sexton** *sehx·tohn*	
17	**sjutton** *sheu·tohn*	
18	**arton** *ar·tohn*	
19	**nitton** *nih·tohn*	
20	**tjugo** *shcheu·goa*	
21	**tjugoett** *shcheu·goa·eht*	

22	**tjugotvå** _shcheu_·goa·tv**oa**
30	**trettio** _treh_·tee·oa
31	**trettioett** _treh_·tee·oa·eht
40	**fyrtio** _fuhr_·tee·oa
50	**femtio** _fehm_·tee·oa
60	**sextio** _sehx_·tee·oa
70	**sjuttio** _sheu_·tee·oa
80	**åttio** _oh_·tee·oa
90	**nittio** _nih_·tee·oa
100	**hundra** _huhn_·dra
101	**hundraett** _huhn_·dra·eht
200	**två hundra** _tvoa_ huhn·dra
500	**fem hundra** _fehm_ huhn·dra
1,000	**ett tusen** eht _teu_·sehn
10,000	**tio tusen** _tee_·oa _teu_·sehn
1,000,000	**en miljon** ehn mihl·_yoan_

Ordinal Numbers

first	**första** _furs_·ta
second	**andra** _an_·dra
third	**tredje** _tree_·dyer
fourth	**fjärde** _fyair_·der
fifth	**femte** _fehm_·ter
once	**en gång** ehn goang
twice	**två gånger** tvoa _goang_·ehr
three times	**tre gånger** tree _goang_·ehr

ESSENTIAL

What time is it?	**Hur mycket är klockan?**	heur <u>mew</u>•ker air <u>kloh</u>•kan
It's noon [midday].	**Klockan är tolv.**	<u>kloh</u>•kan air tolv
Midnight.	**Midnatt.**	<u>meed</u>•nat
From 9 o'clock	**Från nio till sjutton.**	froan <u>nee</u>•oa tihl
to 5 o'clock.		sheu•<u>tohn</u>
It's twenty after [past] four.	**Den är tjugo över fyra.**	dehn air <u>shcheu</u>•goa ur•ver <u>few</u>•ra
It's a quarter to nine.	**Den är kvart i nio.**	dehn air kvart ee <u>nee</u>•oa
5:30 a.m.	**Halv sex på morgonen.**	<u>halv</u> sehx poa <u>mor</u>•oh•nehn
5:30 p.m.	**Halv sex på kvällen.**	<u>halv</u> sehx poa <u>kveh</u>•lehn

Sweden officially follows the 24-hour clock. Formal communication, such as public transporation schedules and TV programming, follows this system. However, in ordinary conversation, time is generally expressed as shown above, often with the addition of **på morgonen** (in the morning), **på förmiddagen** (mid-morning), **på eftermiddagen** (in the afternoon), **på kvällen** (in the evening) and **på natten** (at night).

Days

ESSENTIAL

Monday	**måndag** _moan_·dahg
Tuesday	**tisdag** _tees_·dahg
Wednesday	**onsdag** _oans_·dahg
Thursday	**torsdag** _toash_·dahg
Friday	**fredag** _free_·dahg
Saturday	**lördag** _lurr_·dahg
Sunday	**söndag** _surn_·dahg

Dates

yesterday	**igår** ee·_goar_
today	**idag** ee·_dahg_
tomorrow	**imorgon** ee·_mo_·ron
day	**dag** dahg
week	**vecka** _veh_·ka
month	**månad** _moa_·nad
year	**år** oar

Months

January	**januari** ya·neu·_ah_·ree
February	**februari** fehb·reu·_ah_·ree
March	**mars** mash
April	**april** ap·_rihl_
May	**maj** maiy
June	**juni** _yeu_·nee
July	**juli** _yeu_·lee
August	**augusti** a·_guhss_·tee
September	**september** sehp·_tehm_·behr

October	**oktober** ohk·*toa*·behr
November	**november** noh·*vehm*·behr
December	**december** dee·*sehm*·behr

Sweden follows a day-month-year format instead of the
month-day-year format used in the U.S.
E.g.: July 25, 2008; **25/07/08** = 7/25/2008 in the U.S.

Seasons

spring	**vår** *voar*
summer	**sommar** *soh*·mar
fall [autumn]	**höst** huhst
winter	**vinter** *vihn*·tehr

Holidays

January 1, New Year's Day **Nyårsdagen**
January 6, Epiphany **Trettondagen**
May 1, May Day **Första maj**
June 6, Flag Day **Flaggans dag**
December 25, Christmas Day **Juldagen**
December 26, Boxing Day **Annandag jul**
Moveable dates include:

Good Friday	**Långfredagen**
Ascension	**Kristi himmelfärdsdag**
Whitsunday	**Pingstdagen**
All Saints' Day	**Allhelgonadagen**
Midsummer Day	**Midsommardagen**

The two most important holidays in Sweden are Midsummer and Christmas. **Midsommardagen** (Midsummer) is celebrated with midsummer poles (similar to the may pole) and traditional songs and dances. Traditional food includes **matjesill** (pickled herring), fresh fish and schnapps. For **Juldagen** (Christmas), special cakes and other delicious treats are prepared, such as **pepparkakor** (ginger cookies), **saffranbullar** (saffron buns) and **julbord** (Christmas **smörgåsbord,** a festive buffet). Though not an official holiday, **Luciadagen** (St. Lucia Day) on December 13 marks the beginning of the Chirstmas season. Swedes also celebrate the beginning of spring on April 30, which is known as **Valborgsmässoafton,** with huge bonfires, fireworks and singing. June 6 is **Flaggans dag** (Flag Day), the national day of Sweden. Streets are decorated with yellow and blue, the colors of the Swedish flag, patriotic speeches are made and traditional games and meals are enjoyed.

Conversion Tables

When you know	Multiply by	To find
ounces	28.3	grams
pounds	0.45	kilograms
inches	2.54	centimeters
feet	0.3	meters
miles	1.61	kilometers
square inches	6.45	sq. centimeters
square feet	0.09	sq. meters
square miles	2.59	sq. kilometers
pints (U.S./Brit)	0.47/0.56	liters
gallons (U.S./Brit)	3.8/4.5	liters
Fahrenheit	5/9, after 32	Centigrade
Centigrade	9/5, then +32	Fahrenheit

Kilometers to Miles Conversions

1 km	0.62 miles
5 km	3.1 miles
10 km	6.2 miles
50 km	31 miles
100 km	62 miles

Measurement

1 gram	**gram** *khrahm*	= 0.035 oz.
1 kilogram (kg)	**kilogram** *kee·loa·khrahm*	= 2.2 lb
1 liter (l)	**liter** *lee·tuhr*	= 1.06 U.S./ 0.88 Brit. quarts
1 centimeter (cm)	**centimeter** *sehn·tee· may·tuhr*	= 0.4 inch
1 meter (m)	**meter** *may·tuhr*	= 3.28 feet
1 kilometer (km)	**kilometer** *kee·loa·may·tuhr*	= 0.62 mile

Temperature

	-5° C – 23° F	15° C – 59° F
-40° C – -40° F	-1° C – 30° F	20° C – 68° F
-30° C – -22° F	0° C – 32° F	25° C – 77° F
-20° C – -4° F	5° C – 41° F	30° C – 86° F
-10° C – 14° F	10° C – 50° F	35° C – 95° F

Oven Temperature

100° C – 212° F	177° C – 350° F
121° C – 250° F	204° C – 400° F
149° C – 300° F	260° C – 500° F

Dictionary

English–Swedish 188
Swedish–English 206

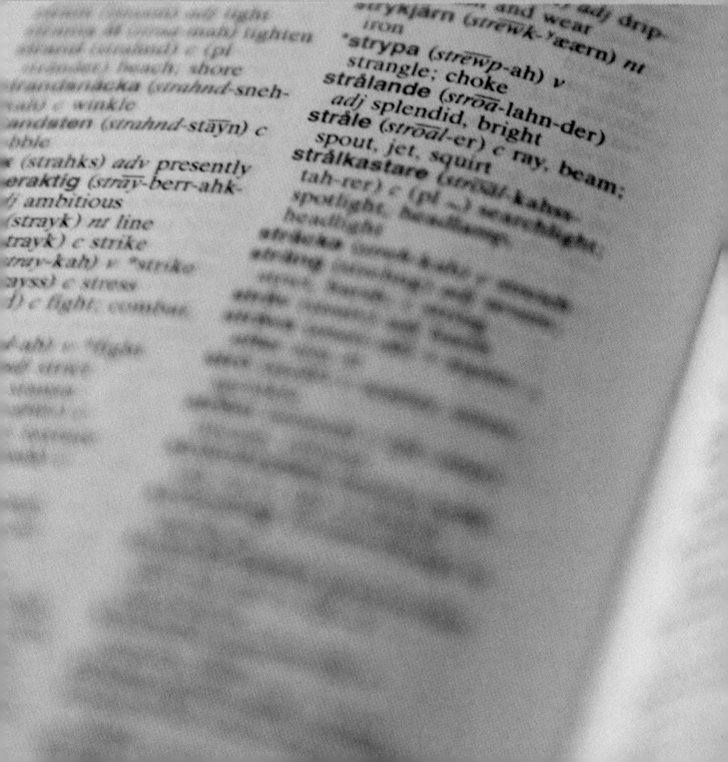

English–Swedish

A

about (approximately) omkring
accept v acceptera
accident olycka
accommodation logi
acetaminophen paracetamol
across över
acupuncture akupunktur
adapter adapter
address n adress
adopt v adoptera
after efter
age ålder
air conditioning luftkonditionering
air mail flygpost
airline flygbolag
airport flygplats
aisle seat plats i mittgången
all alla
allergic allergisk
allergic reaction allergisk reaktion
allergy allergi
allow v tillåta
alter v ändra på
alternate route annan väg

aluminum foil aluminiumfolie
a.m. fm
ambulance ambulans
amount summa
amusement park nöjesfält
and och
anemic anemisk
animal djur
another annan
antiques store antikaffär
antiseptic cream antiseptisk salva
anyone någon
anything något
apartment lägenhet
apologize v be om ursäkt
appliance apparat
approve v godkänna
area code riktnummer
aromatherapy aroma-terapi
arrival ankomst
arrive v anlända
ask v fråga
aspirin huvudvärkstablett
asthma astma
at vid

adj adjective	**BE** British English	**v** verb
adv adverb	**n** noun	

ATM Bankomat
attack *n* anfall
audio guide audioguide
authentic äkta
automatic automatisk
available ledig
away iväg

B

baby baby
baby bottle nappflaska
baby formula välling
baby wipes våtservetter för barn
babysitter barnvakt
backpack ryggsäck
bad dålig
bag (shopping) påse
baggage cart bagagekärra
baggage claim bagageutlämning
bakery bageri
band (music group) band
bandage (gauze) gasbinda
bank bank
bank charge bankavgift
banknote sedel
bar bar
barber herrfrisör
bath bad
bathroom badrum; **(toilet)** toalett
battery batteri
battlefield slagfält

be *v* vara
beach strand
beautiful vacker
become *v* bli
bed *n* säng
before före
begin *v* börja
behind bakom
belt skärp
between mellan
big stor
bicycle cykel
bicycle lock cykelås
bikini bikini
bill *n* **(restaurant bill)** nota; **(hotel, invoice)** räkning
birthday födelsedag
bite *n* bett; *v* **(bite)** bita; *v* **(chew)** tugga
black svart
blanket *n* täcke
bleed *v* blöda
blood blod
blood pressure blodtryck
blouse blus
board *v* **(flight)** borda
boarding house pensionat
boarding pass (airport) boardingkort
boat båt
boat tour båttur

book bok
bookstore bokhandel
boots stövlar
boring trist
botanical garden botanisk trädgård
bottle flaska
bottle opener flasköppnare
bowl djup tallrik
boy pojke
boyfriend pojkvän
bra behå
bracelet armband
break v gå sönder
breakdown v (car) gå sönder
breastfeed v amma
breathe andas
bridge bro
bring ta med
broken (broken) sönder;
  (damaged) trasig
brooch brosch
broom sopborste
brown brun
burn v brinna
bus buss
bus route busslinje
bus station bussterminal
bus stop busshållplats
business center businesscenter
business hours öppettider
business trip affärsresa

busy upptagen
but men
buy v köpa

C

cabin stuga
cafe kafé
calender kalender
call v (phone) ringa
calm lugn
camera kamera
camping bed tältsäng
can n burk; v (be able to) kan
can opener konservöppnare
cancel v avbeställa
car bil
car deck (ferry) bildäck
car ferry bilfärja
car park [BE] parkeringsplats
car rental biluthyrning
car seat bilbarnstol
carafe karaff
card n kort
carry on n (luggage) handbagage
cash kontant
cashier (male) kassör; **(female)**
  kassörska
casino kasino
castle slott
cathedral katedral
cave grotta

cell phone mobiltelefon
ceramics keramik
certificate of authenticity
   äkthetsbevis
chair lift stollift
change *n* **(money)** växel; *v*
   (transportation; a baby) byta; *v*
   (reservation) ändra;
cheap billig
check in *v* checka in
check in desk (airport) incheckning
check out *v* checka ut
checking account checkkonto
chemical toilet kemisk toalett
chemist [BE] apotek
chest bröstet
child barn
child's cot [BE] barnsäng
children's menu barnmeny
church kyrka
cigar cigarr
cinema [BE] bio
city (city) stad; **(downtown)**
   centrum
city map stadskarta
classical music klassiskmusik
clean *n* ren
cleaning supplies städutrustning
clear *v* **(computer)** rensa
cliff klippa
cling film [BE] plastfolie

clock klocka
close *v* stänga
closed stängt
clothing store klädaffär
coat rock
coffee shop konditori
coin mynt
cold (illness) förskylning;
   (temperature) kall
colleague kollega
color färg
comb kam
come *v* komma
company (business) firma;
   (companionship) sällskap
computer dator
concert konsert
conditioner hårbalsam
condom kondom
conference konferens
conference room konferensrum
confirm *v* **(reservation)** bekräfta
contact lens solution
   kontaktlinsvätska
contain *v* innehålla
contraceptive preventivmedel
convention hall kongresshall
cooking facilities kokmöjligheter
cool (temperature) sval
copy *n* kopia
copy machine kopieringsautomat

corkscrew korkskruv
correct rätt
cost v kosta
cotton bomull
cough n hosta; v hosta
country code landsnummer
cover charge kuvertavgift
credit card kreditkort
crib barnsäng
cross country skiing längdåkning
crystal (glass) kristallglas
cup kopp
culture kultur
currency valuta
currency exchange office
   växelkontor
customs tull
customs declaration form
   tulldeklaration
cute adj gullig
cycling cykelåkning

D

dala horse dalahäst
damage v (damage) skada; n
   (harm) skada
dance v dansa
dance club diskotek
day ticket dagsbiljett
day trip dagstur
deaf döv

debit card bankkort
declare v (customs) förtulla
deck chair solstol
deep djup
delay n försening
delete v (computer) radera
delicatessen delikatessaffär
denim denim
dentist tandläkare
denture tandprotes
deodorant deodorant
depart v (train) avgå
department store varuhus
departure (airport) avgång
departure gate avgångsgate
deposit handpenning
desire adj gärna; n lust
detour trafikomläggning
develop v (photos) framkalla
diabetic n diabetiker
dial v (number) slå
diamond diamant
diaper blöja
diarrhea diarré
diesel diesel
difficult svårt
digital digital
digital print digitalt kort
dirty smutsig
disabled rörelsehindrad
disabled accessible toilet [BE]

handicappanpassad toalett
discount rabatt
discount card rabattkort
dish detergent diskmedel
dishwasher diskmaskin
display case vitrin
disposable camera engångskamera
disturb v störa
dive v dyka
divide v dela
diving equipment dykarutrustning
divorced skild
dizzy yr
do v (do something) göra; (work with) syssla med
do not disturb var god stör ej
doctor doktor
doll docka
dollar dollar
domestic (travel) inrikes
domestic flight inrikes flyg
domestic partner sambo
door dörr
dosage dosering
downtown centrum
dress klänning
dress code klädsel
drive v köra
driver's license körkort
drops (medication) droppar
dry cleaner kemtvätt

dubbed dubbad
duty free taxfri
duty free good taxfri vara

E

each varje
ear öra
earring örhänge
east öster
easy lätt
eat v äta
economy class turist klass
electrical outlet nätuttag
elevator hiss
e-mail e-post
e-mail address e-postadress
emergency nödsituation
emergency brake nödbroms
emergency exit nödutgång
English engelska
engrave v gravera
enter n (entrance) ingång; (computer) enter
entertainment underhållning
equipment utrustning
escalator rulltrappa
e-ticket e-biljett
European Union (EU) europeiska unionen
event händelse
examine v (medical) undersöka

excess baggage överviktsbagage
exchange rate växelkursen
excuse me (attention, pardon) ursäkta; **(to get past)** ursäkta mig
exit *n* **(way out)** utgång
expensive dyr
expert avancerad
express express
express mail expresspost
extension (phone) anknytning
eyeglasses glasögon

F

fabric tyg
family familj
fan (ventilation) fläkt
fantastic *adj* fantastisk
fare biljettpris
farm bondgård
fast fort
fax fax
fax machine fax machine
female kvinna
ferry färja
fever feber
field fält
fill *v* **(prescription)** göra i ordning
filling (dental) plomb
film [BE] film
fire exit brandutgång
first första

fishing fiske
fit *v* **(clothing)** passa
fitting room provrum
fix *v* laga
fixed price fast pris
flat [BE] lägenhet
flight flyg
flight number flygnummer
floor (level) våning
football [BE] fotboll
for (someone) för
foreign currency utländsk valuta
forest skog
forget *v* glömma
fork gaffel
form *n* blankett
fountain fontän
free (available) ledig
free of charge gratis
freezer frys
friend vän
from ifrån
frying pan stekpanna
fun rolig
function *v* **(work)** fungera
further (more) ytterligare

G

game spel
garbage sopor
garbage bag soppåse

gasoline bensin
gas station bensinstation
gate (boarding) gate
genuine äkta
get off (train) stiga av
gift shop presentaffär
gift present
girlfriend flickvän
give *v* ge
glass (drinking) glas
gold guld
golf golf
golf club golfklubba
golf course golfbana
good *adj* bra
goodbye hej då
greengrocer [BE] livsmedelsaffär
grocery store livsmedelsaffär
group grupp
guest gäst
guide (brochure) guide; (person) guide
guide dog ledarhund
gym gym

H

hair cut klippning
hair dryer hårtork
hair style frisyr
hairbrush hårborste
hairdresser damfrisör

hairspray hårspray
half halv
handbag [BE] handväska
handicapped rörelsehindrade
handicapped accessible toilet handicappanpassad toalett
handicraft hantverk
handmade handgjord
hat hatt
have *v* ha
health food store hälsokostaffär
hearing impaired hörselskadad
heat värme
helmet hjälm
help *n* hjälp; *v* hjälpa
here här
hi hej
highchair barnstol
highway motorväg
hike *v* vandra
hiking vandring
hill kulle
hire *v* [BE] rent
holiday [BE] (vacation) semester
holiday (celebration) helgdag
horseback riding ridsport
hospital sjukhus
hot varm
hotel hotell
hour timme
husband man

I

ibuprofen ibuprofen
ice hockey ishockey
identification (idenitification) legitimation; **(ID card)** ID-kort
ill [BE] sjuk
in i
included (in the price) inkluderad
indoor pool inomhusbassäng
information desk information
innocent oskyldig
insect insekt
insect bite insektbett
insect repellent mygg olja
inside inuti
instant messenger instant messenger
instructor instruktör
insurance försäkring
interesting intressant
international (travel) utrikes
international driver's license internationellt körkort
internet internet
internet cafe internetkafé
interpreter tolk
iron *n* **(clothes)** strykjärn; *v* **(clothes)** stryka
itemized bill specificerad räkning

J

jacket jacka
jeans jeans
jet ski jetski
jeweler juvelerare
jewelry smycken
job jobb

K

keep *v* behålla
key nyckel
key card nyckelkort
kiddie pool barnbassäng
kiss *v* kyssa
kitchen kök
knife kniv
krona (Swedish currency) krona

L

lace spets
lactose intolerant laktosinterant
ladies' restroom damtoilett
ladieswear damkläder
lake sjö
last sista
late sen
launderette [BE] snabbtvätt
laundromat snabbtvätt
laundry tvätt
laundry detergent tvättmedel
laundry facilities tvättmöjligheter

lawyer advokat
leather läder
leave *v* lämna
left (direction) vänster
lesson lektion
letter brev
library bibliotek
life boat livbåt
life jacket flytväst
lifeguard livräddare
lift (ski) lift
lift [BE] *n* **(elevator)** hiss
lift pass liftkort
light (lamp) lampa
light bulb glödlampa
lighter tändare
like *v* gilla
line (bus) linje
linen linne
live *v* bo
loafers loafers
lock *v* låsa
log on logga in
log out logga ut
long *adj* lång; *adv* länge
lose *v* **(lost luggage)** förlora; *v*
  (drop, lose) tappa
lost *n* vilse
lost property office [BE]
  hittegodsexpedition
lost and found hittegodsexpedition

lottery lotto
love *v* älska
luggage locker förvaringsskåp

M

mail post
mailbox postlåda
manager chef
manicure manikyr
many många
map karta
market marknad
married gift
mass mässan
match (fire) tändsticka
meal måltid
mean *v* **(signify)** betyda
measuring spoon måttsked
medicine medicin
medium medium
meet *v* träffa
meeting sammanträde
memory card minneskort
men's restroom herrtoalett
menstrual cramps mensvärk
menstruation mens
menswear herrkläder
menu meny
message meddelande
microwave mikrovågsugn
minimum minimum

Miss fröken
mistake misstag
mobile phone [BE] mobiltelefon
moment ögonblick
mop *n* skurmop
moped moped
mosque moské
motel motell
motion sickness åksjuka
motorboat motorbåt
motorcycle motocykel
motorway [BE] motorväg
mountain berg
mouth mun
movie film
movies bio
Mr. herr
Mrs. fru
mugging överfall
multi-day card flerdagskort
museum museum
must måste

N

nail file nagelfil
nail salon nagelvårdssalong
name *n* namn
napkin servett
nappy [BE] blöja
nature reserve naturreservat
nearby nära

necklace halsband
need *v* behöva
new ny
newspaper tidning
newsstand tidningskiosk
next nästa
next to bredvid
nice *adj* snäll
no (not allowed) ej
nobody ingen
no smoking rökning förbjuden
north norr
not inte
not included (in the price) inte
   inkluderad
nothing inget
number nummer
nurse sjuksköterska

O

off av
old gammal
on (switch) på
one way (street) enkelriktad
one-way ticket enkel biljett
only bara
open *n* öppet; *v* öppna
opening hours [BE] öppettider
opera opera
opposite mitt emot
optician optiker

or eller
orchestra orkester
order v beställa
other andra
outdoor utomhus
outdoor pool utomhusbassäng
outside ute
overnight delivery (mail)
  expressutdelning
oxygen treatment syrebehandling

P

pacifier napp
package paket
paddling pool [BE] barnbassäng
pajamas pyjamas
panorama panorama
pants byxor
panty hose strumpbyxor
paper napkin papperservett
parcel [BE] paket
park n park; v parkera
parking parkering
parking lot parkeringsplats
passport pass
passport control passkontroll
password (computer) lösenord
pay phone telefonautomat
pay v betala
peak (mountain) top
pearl pärla

pedestrian crossing
  övergångsställe för fotgängare
pedestrian fotgängare
pedicure pedikyr
pen kulspetspenna
per per
per day per dag
per week per vecka
performance (music, theater)
  föreställning
person person
petite petit
petrol [BE] bensin
petrol station [BE] bensinstation
pewter tenn
pharmacy apotek
phone call samtal
phone card telefonkort
phone number telefonnummer
photo foto
pick up v (person/thing) hämta
picnic area picknickområde
piece bit
pill tablett
pillow kudde
PIN PIN kod
pink rosa
piste [BE] spår
place n ställe
plan n plan
plaster [BE] plåster

plastic wrap plastfolie
platform (train) plattform
platinum platina
plate tallrik
play n (theater) teaterpjäs; v spela
playground lekplats
playpen lekrum
pleasant trevlig
please (request) snälla; (invitation) varsågod
plunger vaskrensare
pocket n ficka
point of interest sevärdhet
police polis
police report polisrapport
police station polisstation
pond damm
post office postkontor
postage porto
postcard vykort
pot (cooking pot) gryta; (saucepan) kastrull
pound sterling engelsk pund
pregnant gravid
premium (gas) premium
prescription recept
price pris
print (computer) skriva ut
private privat
private room privatrum
problem problem

produce store matbutik
program (events) program
pub pub
public transportation allmänna kommunikationer
pull dra
purple lila
purpose syfte
purse (large) handväska, (small) portmonnä
push tryck
pushchair [BE] sittvagn

R

racket (tennis) racket
railroad järnväg
railway [BE] järnväg
rain regn
raincoat regnkappa
rap rap
rape n våldtäkt
rapids fors
rash n utslag
(disposable) razor (engångs) rakhyvel
reach v nå
read v läsa
ready färdig
receipt kvitto
receive v ta emot
receptionist receptionist

recommend *v* rekommendera
refrigderator kylskåp
region region
regular gas vanlig
relationship (romantic)
  förhållande
rent *n* hyra; *v* hyra
repair *v* reparera
repairs (car) reparationer
repeat *v* upprepa
report *v* **(crime)** anmäla
reservation bokning
reserved reserverad
rest area rastplats
restroom (sign) WC
restaurant restaurang
return *v* **(give back)** återlämna
return ticket [BE] retur (biljett)
reverse charge call [BE] ba- samtal
right (correct) rätt; **(direction)**
  höger
ring (jewelry) ring
river flod
road väg
road map vägkarta
romantic romantisk
room rum
room service rumservice
round *n* **(golf)** runda
round-trip ticket retur biljett
rubbish [BE] sopor

S

safe *n* kassaskåp
sailing segling
sandals sandaler
sanitary napkin binda
saucepan kastrull
sauna bastu
save *v* **(collect)** spara
scarf halsduk
schedule tidsschema
scissors sax
sea hav
seat (on train) plats
seat number platsnummer
seat reservation (train)
  sittplatsbiljett
seminar seminarium
send *v* skicka
separated (couple) separerad
service serveringsavgift
service charge (bank)
  expeditionsavgift
sex sex
shampoo shampoo
sheet lakan
shoe store skoaffär
shoes skor
shopping basket shoppingkorg
shopping cart shoppingvagn
shopping centre [BE]
  shoppingcenter

shopping mall shoppingcenter
shorts shorts
show v visa
shower dusch
sick sjuk
side effect biverkning
sightseeing tour sightseeingtur
sign v undertäckna
silk siden
SIM card (cell phone) SIM kort
single ticket [BE] enkel **(biljett)**
sit v sitta
size storlek
skiing skidåkning
skirt kjol
slice n skiva
slippers tofflor
slippery (icy) hal
slow adj långsam
small liten
sneakers träningsskor
snorkeling equipment
   snorkelutrustning
snow snö
snowboard snowboard
snowshoes pjäxor
soap tvål
soccer fotboll
sock socka
something något
soon snart

soother [BE] napp
sore throat halsont
sorry förlåt
south söder
souvenir souvenir
spa spa
spatula stekspade
speak v tala
spoon sked
sports massage träningsmassage
spouse (female) maka; **(male)**
   make
sprain stukning
square (town feature) torg
stadium stadion
stair trappa
stamp n frimärke
stamp your ticket stämpla er biljett
start v **(car)** starta
stay n stanna
steakhouse stekhus
steep brant
stolen stulen
stomach magen
stomachache ont i magen
stop n **(bus stop)** bushållplats; v
   stanna
store n butik; v förvara
strange konstig
stream å
street gata

stroller sittvagn
student studerande
study v läsa
stunning jättesnygg
subtitle text
suburb förort
subway tunnelbana
subway station tunnelbanestation
suitable lämplig
suitcase resväska
sunburn solbränna
sunglasses solglasögon
sunstroke solsting
super [BE] (gas) premium
supermarket snabbköp
surfboard surfbräda
sweater tröja
sweatshirt sweatshirt
Swedish adj svensk; **(language)**
  svenska
swelling svullnad
swim v simma
swimming pool simbassäng
swimming trunks badbyxor
swimsuit baddräkt
symbol (computer) tecken
symphony (orchestra) symfoni
synagogue synagoga

T
table bord

tablecloth duk
take v ta
take out v ta ut
taken (occupied) upptagen
tampon tampong
tax skatt
taxi taxi
teaspoon tesked
temperature temperatur
temple tempel
tennis tennis
tennis court tennisbana
terminal (airport) terminal
terrible förskräcklig
text message sms
textiles textil
thank you tack
theft rån
thief tjuv
think v tänka
ticket biljett
ticket machine biljettautomat
ticket office biljettkontor
tie n slips
tights [BE] strumpbyxor
timetable [BE] tidsschema
tip (service) dricks
tissue näsduk
to till
tobacconist tobaksaffär
toilet [BE] toalett; **(sign)** WC

toilet paper toalettpapper
tooth tand
toothbrush tandborste
toothpaste tandkräm
tour tur
tourist turist
tourist attraction turistattraktion
tourist information
  turistinformation
tourist office turistbyrå
town hall stadshus
toy store leksaksaffär
track (railroad) spår
trail spår
train n tåg
train station järnvägsstation
tram spårvagn
translate v översätta
travel v (travel) resa; (drive) åka
travel agency resebyrå
travel agent (female)
  resebyråkvinna; (male)
  resebyråman
travel sickness [BE] åksjuka
traveler's check resecheck
traveller's cheque [BE] resecheck
treat v (to a meal) bjuda
trim (hair) putsning
trip n resa
trolley [BE] bagagekärra
trouser [BE] byxor

try v prova
turn off v stänga av
turn on v sätta på

U

ugly ful
umbrella (standard) paraply; (sun)
  solparasol
underground [BE] tunnelbana
underground station [BE]
  tunnelbanestation
understand v förstå
underwear (general) underkläder
unfortunately tyvärr
United Kingdom Storbritanien
unlimited (mileage) obegränsad
until tills
urgent brådskande
United State Förenta Staterna
use v använda
username användarnamn
utensil bestick

V

vacancy ledigt rum
vacation semester
vacuum cleaner dammsugare
vaginal infection vaginal infektion
valley dal
valuable värdesak
value n värde

vegetarian vegetarian
viewpoint utsiktspunkt
village by
visit *n* besök; *v* besöka
visiting hours besökstid
visitor besökare
visitor besökare
visually impaired syn skadad
vomit *v* kräkas

W

wait vänta
wake up *v* vakna
wake-up call telefonväckning
walk *n* promenad; *v* gå
wallet plånbok
want *v* vilja
washing machine tvättmaskin
waterfall vattenfall
weather forecast väderleksrapport
weekend helg
welcome välkommen
west väster
wheelchair rullstol
wheelchair ramp rullstolsramp
when när
where var
which vilken
white vitt
who vem

widow änka
widower änkling
window fönster
window seat fönsterplats
windsurfing vindsurfa
wireless internet trådlös internet
with med
withdrawal (bank) uttag
wood trä
wool ull
work from home *v* arbeta hemifrån
wrap *v* **(present)** slå in
write *v* skriva
wrong fel

Y

yellow gul
yes ja
yield lämna företräde
youth hostel vandrarhem

Z

zoo djurpark

Swedish–English

A

acceptera *v* accept
adapter adapter
adoptera *v* adopt
adress *n* address
advokat lawyer
affärscentrum shopping mall [centre BE]
affärsresa business trip
akupunktur acupuncture
alla all
allergi allergy
allergisk allergic
allergisk reaktion allergic reaction
allmänna kommunikationer public transportation
alternativ väg alternate route
aluminiumfolie aluminum foil
ambulans ambulance
amma *v* breastfeed
andas breathe
andra other
anemisk anemic
anfall *n* attack
anknytning extension (phone)
ankomst arrival
anlända *v* arrive
anmäla *v* report (crime)

annan another
antikaffär antiques store
antiseptisk salva antiseptic cream
använda *v* use
användarnamn username
apotek pharmacy [chemist BE]
apparat appliance
arbeta hemifrån *v* work from home
armband bracelet
aroma-terapi aromatherapy
astma asthma
audioguide audio guide
automatisk automatic
av off
avancerad expert
avbeställa *v* cancel
avgå *v* depart (plane)
avgång departure
avgångsgate departure gate

B

baby baby
bad bath
badbyxor swim trunks
baddräkt swim suit
badrum bathroom [toilet BE]
bagagekärra baggage cart [trolley BE]
bagageutlämning baggage claim

bageri bakery
bakom behind
band band (music group)
bank bank
bankavgift bank charge
bankkort debit card
Bankomat ATM
bar bar
bara only (just)
barn child
barnbassäng kiddie pool [paddling pool BE]
barnmeny children's menu
barnstol highchair
barnsäng crib [child's cot BE]
barnvakt babysitter
bastu sauna
batteri battery
be om ursäkt *v* apologize
behå bra
behålla *v* keep
behöva *v* need
bekräfta *v* confirm (reservation)
bensin gasoline [petrol BE]
bensinstation gas station [petrol station BE]
berg mountain
bergklättring rock climbing
bestick utensil
beställa *v* order
besök *n* visit

besöka *v* visit
besökare visitor
besökstid visiting hours
betala *v* pay
bett *n* bite
betyda mean (signify)
bibliotek library
bikini bikini
bil car
bilbarnstol car seat
bildäck car deck (ferry)
bilfärja car ferry
biljett ticket
biljettautomat ticket machine
biljettkontor ticket office
biljettpris fare
billig cheap
bilsäte car seat
biluthyrning car rental
binda sanitary napkin [towel BE]
bio movies [cinema BE]
bit piece
bita *v* bite
biverkning side effect
bjuda *v* treat (to a meal)
blankett *n* form
bli *v* become
blod blood
blodtryck blood pressure
blus blouse
blöda bleed

blöja diaper [nappy BE]
bo v live
boardingkort boarding pass
bok book
bokhandel bookstore
bokning reservation (travel, restaurant)
bomull cotton
bondgård farm
bord table
borda v board (flight)
botanisk trädgård botanical garden
bra adj good
brandutgång fire exit
brant steep
bredvid next to
brev letter
brinna v burn
bro bridge
brosch brooch
brun brown
brådskande urgent
bröstet chest
burk n can
businesscenter business center
buss bus
busshållplats bus stop [request stop BE]
busslinje bus route
bussterminal bus station
butik n store

by village
byta v change (baby, connection)
byxor pants [trouser BE]
båt boat
båttur boat tour
börja v begin

C

centrum downtown
checka in check in (airport)
checka ut check out (hotel)
chef manager
cigarr cigar
cykel bicycle
cykelåkning cycling
cykelås bicycle lock

D

dagsbiljett day ticket
dagstur day trip
dal valley
dalahäst dala horse
damfrisör hairdresser
damkläder ladieswear
damtoalett ladies' restroom
damm pond
dammsugare vacuum cleaner
dansa v dance
dator computer
dela divide
delikatessaffär delicatessen

denim denim
deodorant deodorant
diabetiker *n* diabetic
diamant diamond
diarré diarrhea
diesel diesel
digital digital
digitalt kort digital print
diskmedel dish detergent
diskmaskin dishwasher
djup deep
djup tallrik bowl
djur animal
djurpark zoo
docka doll
doktor doctor
dollar dollar
dosering dosage
dra pull
dricks tip (service)
droppar drops (medication)
dubbad dubbed
duk table cloth
dusch shower
dyka *v* dive
dykarutrustning diving equipment
dyr expensive
dålig bad
dörr door
döv deaf

E

e-biljett e-ticket
efter after
ej no (do not…)
eller or
endast only (nothing but)
engelska English
engelsk pund pound sterling
engångskamera disposable camera
enkel biljett one-way trip [single ticket BE]
enkelriktad one way (street)
enter enter (computer)
e-post e-mail
e-postadress e-mail address
europeiska unionen European Union (EU)
expeditionsavgift service charge (bank)
express express
expresspost express mail
expressutdelning overnight delivery (mail)

F

familj family
fantastisk *adj* fantastic
fast pris fixed price
fax fax
fax machine fax machine
feber fever

fel wrong
ficka *n* pocket
film movie [film BE]
fiske fishing
flaska bottle
flasköppnare bottle opener
flerdagskort multi-day card
flickvän girlfriend
flod river
flyg flight
flygbolag airline
flygnummer flightnumber
flygplats airport
flygpost airmail
fläkt fan
fm a.m.
fontän fountain
fors rapids
fort fast
fotboll soccer [football BE]
fotgängare pedestrian
foto photo
framkalla *v* develop (photos)
fri free
frimärken stamps
frisyr hair style
fru Mrs.
frys freezer
fråga ask
från from…
fröken Miss

ful ugly
fungera *v* function (work)
fylla *v* fill
fält field
färdig ready
färg color
färja ferry
födelsedag birthday
fönster window
fönsterplats window seat
för tung/stor too much, excess (baggage)
före before
Förenta Staterna United States
föreställning performance (music, theater)
förhållande relationship (romantic)
förlora *v* lose
förlåt sorry
försening *n* delay
förskräcklig terrible
förskylning cold (sick)
första first
förstå *v* understand
försäkring insurance
förtulla *v* declare (customs)
förvaringsskåp luggage locker
förort suburb

G

gaffel fork

gammal *adj* old, *n* age
gasbinda bandage (gauze)
gata street
gate gate (boarding)
ge *v* give
gift married
gilla *v* like
glas glass (drinking)
glasögon eyeglasses
glödlampa light bulb
glömma *v* forget
godkänna *v* approve
golf golf
golfbana golf course
golfklubb golf club
gratis free of charge
gravera *v* engrave
gravid pregnant
grotta cave
grupp group
gryta pot (cooking)
guide guide (brochure); guide (person)
gul yellow
guld gold
gullig *adj* cute
gym gym
gå *v* walk, leave
gå sönder break; breakdown (car)
gärna *adj* desire
göra *v* do

H

ha *v* have
hal slippery (icy)
halsband necklace
halsduk scarf
halsont sore throat
halv halv
handbagage carry on
handgjord handmade
handicappanpassad toalett handicapped accessible toilet [disabled BE]
handpenning deposit
handväska purse [hand bag BE]
hantverk handicraft
hatt hat
hav sea
hej hi
hej då goodbye
helg weekend
helgdag holiday (celebration)
hemifrån work from home
hemlagad homemade (food)
herr Mr.
herrfrisör barber
herrkläder menswear
herrtoalett men's restroom
iss elevator [lift BE]
hittegodsexpedition lost-and-found [lost property office BE]
hjälm helmet

hjälp *n* help
hjälpa *v* help
hosta *n* cough; *v* to cough
hotell hotel
huvudvärkstablett aspirin
hyra rent [hire BE]
hårbalsam conditioner
hårborste hairbrush
hårspray hairspray
hårtork hair dryer
hälsokostaffär health food store
hämta *v* pick up (thing/person)
händelse event
här here
höger right (direction)
hörselskadad hearing impaired

I

i in
ibuprofen ibuprofen
ID-kort identification
ifrån from
incheckning check in desk (airport)
information information desk
ingen nobody (sg)
inget nothing
ingång entrance
inkluderad included (in the price)
innehålla contain
inomhusbassäng indoor swimming pool

inrikes domestic (travel)
inrikes flyg domestic flight
insekt insect
insektbett insect bite
instant messenger instant messenger
instruktör instructor
inte not
inte inkluderad not included (in the price)
internationellt
körkort international driver's license
internet internet
internetkafé internet café
intressant interesting
inuti inside
ishockey ice hockey
iväg away

J

ja yes
jacka jacket
jeans jeans
jetski jet ski
jobb job
juvelerare jeweler
järnväg railroad [railway BE]
järnvägsstation train station
jättesnygg stunning

kafé café
kalender calendar
kall cold (temperature)
kam comb
kamera camera
kan v can (be able to)
karaff carafe
karta map
kasino casino
kassaskåp n safe
kassör cashier (male)
kassörska cashier (female)
kastrull saucepan (cooking)
katedral cathedral
kemisk toalett chemical toilet
kemtvätt dry cleaner
keramik ceramics
kjol skirt
klassiskmusik classical music
klippa cliff
klippning hair cut
klocka(n) clock
klädaffär clothing store
klädsel dress code
klänning dress
kniv knife
kokmöjligheter cooking facilities
kollega colleague
komma v come
konditori coffee shop

kondom condom
konferens conference
konferensrum conference room
kongresshall convention hall
konsert concert
konservöppnare can opener
konstig strange
kontaktlinsvätska contact lens solution
kontant n cash
kopia n copy
kopieringsautomat copy machine
kopp cup
korkskruv corkscrew
kort n card, adj short
kosta v cost
kostym suit (jacket/pants)
kreditkort credit card
kristallglas crystal (glass)
krona krona (Swedish currency)
kräkas v vomit
kudde pillow
kulle hill
kulspetspenna pen
kultur culture
kuvertavgift cover charge
kvinna female
kvitto receipt
kylskåp refridgerator
kyrka church
kyssa v kiss

kök kitchen
köpa v buy
köra drive
körkort driver's license

L

laga v fix
lakan sheet
laktosintolerant lactose intolerant
lampa light (lamp)
landsnummer country code
ledarhund guide dog
ledig available
ledigt rum vacancy
legitimation identification
lekplats playground
lekrum playpen
leksaksaffär toy store
lektion lesson
liftkort liftpass
lila purple
linje line
linne linen
liten small
livbåt life boat
livräddare lifeguard
livsmedelsaffär grocery store
  [greengrocer BE]
loafers loafers
logga in log on (connect to internet)
logga ut log out

logi accommodation
lotto lottery
luftkonditionering air conditioning
lugn calm
lust n desire
lyft lift (ski)
lång long
långsam slow
låsa v lock
läder leather
lägenhet apartment [flat BE]
lämna v leave
lämna före träde yield
lämplig suitable
längdåkning cross country skiing
länge long (time)
läsa v (book) read; (school) study
lätt easy
lösenord password

M

magen stomach
maka spouse (female)
make spouse (male)
man husband, man
manikyr manicure
marknad market
matbutik produce store (general
  store) [grocer BE]
med with
meddelande message

medicin medicine
medium medium
mellan between
men but
mens menstruation
mensvärk menstrual cramps
meny menu
mikrovågsugn microwave
minimum minimum (requirement)
minneskort memory card
misstag mistake
mitt emot opposite
mobiltelefon cell phone [mobile phone BE]
moms sales tax [VAT BE]
moped moped
moské mosque
motel motel
motorcykel motorcycle
motorbåt motorboat
motorväg highway [motorway BE]
mun mouth
museum museum
mygg olja insect repellent
mynt coin
måltid meal
många many
måste must
måttsked measuring spoon
mässan mass (catholic)

N

nagelfil nail file
nagelvårdssalong nail salon
namn *n* name
napp pacifier [soother BE]
nappflaska baby bottle
naturreservat nature reserve
norr north
nota bill (restaurant)
nummer number
ny new
nyckel key
nyckelkort key card
nå *v* reach
någon anyone
något anything, something
när when
nära nearby
näsduk tissue
nästa next
nätuttag electrical outlet
nödbroms emergency brake
nödsituation emergency
nödutgång emergency exit
nöjesfält amusement park

O

obegränsad unlimited (mileage)
och and
olycka accident
omkring about (approximately)

ont i magen stomachache
opera opera
optiker optician
orkester orchestra

P

paket package [parcel BE]
panorama panorama
papperservett paper napkin
paracetamol acetaminophen
paraply umbrella
park park
parkering parking
parkering på gatan street parking
parkeringsplats (one or several)
   parking lot [car park BE]
pass passport
passa v fit
passkontroll passport control
pedikyr pedicure
pensionat boarding house
per per
per dag per day
per vecka per week
person person
petit petite
picknickområde picnic area
PIN kod PIN code
pjäxor snowshoes
plan n plan
plastfolie plastic wrap [cling film BE]

platina platinum
plats seat (on train)
plats i mittgången aisle seat
platsnummer seat number
plattform platform (train)
plomb filling
plånbok wallet
pojke boy
pojkvän boyfriend
polis police
polisrapport police report
polisstation police station
porto postage
post mail
postkontor post office
postlåda mail box
premium premium [super BE] (gas)
presentaffär gift shop
present gift
preventivmedel contraceptive
pris price
privat private
privatrum private room
problem problem
program progam (events)
prova v try
provrum fitting room
pub pub
putsning trim (hair)
pyjamas pajamas
på on (switch)

påse bag
pärla pearl

R

rabatt discount
rabattkort discount card
racket racket (tennis)
radera delete (computer)
(engångs)rakhyvel (disposable) razor
rap rap
rastplats rest area
recept prescription
receptionist receptionist
region region
regn rain
regnkappa raincoat
rekommendera v recommend
ren adj clean
rensa clear (computer, ATM), clean
reparationer repairs (car)
reparera v repair
resa v travel, n trip
resebyrå travel agency
resebyråkvinna travel agent (female)
resebyråman travel agent (male)
resecheck traveler's check [traveller's cheque BE]
reserverad reserved
restaurang restaurant

resväska suitcase
retur (biljett) round-trip ticket [return ticket BE]
ridsport horseback riding
riktnummer area code
ring ring (jewelry)
ringa v call (phone)
rock coat
rolig fun
romantisk romantic
rosa pink
rullstol wheelchair
rullstolsramp wheelchair ramp
rulltrappa escalator
rum room
rumservice room service
runda v round (golf)
ryggsäck backpack
rån theft
räkning bill (hotel, invoice)
rätt correct
rökning förbjuden no smoking
rörelsehindrad disabled

S

sambo domestic partner
sammanträde meeting
samtal phone call
sandaler sandals
sax scissors
sedel banknote

segling sailing
semester vacation
seminarium seminar
sen late
separerad separated (couple)
serveringsavgift service
servett napkin
sevärdhet point of interest
sex sex
shampoo shampoo
shoppingcenter shopping mall
 [shopping centre BE]
shoppingkorg shopping basket
shoppingvagn shopping cart
shorts shorts
siden silk
sightseeingtur sightseeing tour
simbassäng swimming pool
SIM kort SIM card (cell phone)
simma v swim
sista last
sitta v sit
sittplatsbiljett seat reservation
 (train)
sittvagn stroller [pushchair BE]
sjuk sick [ill BE]
sjukhus hospital
sjuksköterska nurse
sjö lake
skada n damage, v harm
skatt tax

sked spoon
skicka v send
skidåkning skiing
skild divorced
skiva n slice
skoaffär shoe store
skog forest
skor shoes
skriva write
skriva ut print
skurmop n mop
skyldig innocent
skärp belt
slagfält battlefield
slips tie
slott castle
slå v (phone number) dial
slå in v wrap (present)
sms text message
smutsig dirty
smycken jewelry
snabbköp supermarket
snabbtvätt Laundromat
 [launderette BE]
snart soon
snorkelutrustning snorkeling
 equipment
snowboard snowboard
snäll adj nice
snälla (request) please
snö snow

socka sock
solbränna sunburn
solglasögon sunglasses
solsting sunstroke
solstol deck chair
sopborste broom
sopor garbage (garbage disposal) [rubbish BE]
soppåse garbage bag
souvenir souvenir
spa spa
spara *v* save
specifierad räkning itemized bill
spel game
spela *v* play
spets lace
spår trail [piste BE]; track (railroad)
spårvagn tram
stad city
stadion stadium
stadshus town hall
stadskarta city map
stanna *n* stay; *v* stop
starta *v* start
stekhus steakhouse
stekpanna frying pan
stekspade spatula
stiga av get off (train)
stollift chair lift
stor big
Storbritannien United Kingdom

storlek size
strand beach
strumpbyxor panty hose [tights BE]
strykjärn iron (clothes)
studerande student
stuga cabin
stukning *n* sprain
stulen stolen
städutrustning cleaning supplies
ställe place
stämpla er biljett stamp your ticket
stäng av turn off
stänga *v* close
stängt closed
störa disturb
stövlar boots
summa amount
surfbräda surfboard
sval cool (temperature)
svart black
sweatshirt sweatshirt
svensk *adj* swedish
svenska *adj* swedish; (language) Swedish
svullnad swelling
svårt difficult
syfte purpose
symfoni symphony (orchestra)
syn skadad visually impaired
synagoga synagogue
syrebehandling oxygen treatment

syssla med v do (work with)
sällskap company (companionship)
säng bed
sätta på turn on
söder south
sönder broken

T

ta v take
ta emot v receive
ta med bring
ta ut take out
tablett pill (tablet)
tack thank you
tala v speak
tallrik plate
tampong tampon
tand tooth
tandborste toothbrush
tandkräm toothpaste
tandläkare dentist
tandprotes dentures
tappa v lose; drop
taxfri duty free
taxfri vara duty free good
taxi taxi
teaterpjäs play (theater)
tecken symbol (computer)
telefon katalog telephone catalog
telefonautomat pay phone
telefonkort phone card

telefonnummer phone number
telefonväckning wake up call
temperatur temperature
tempel temple
tenn pewter
tennis tennis
tennisbana tennis court
terminal terminal (airport)
tesked teaspoon
text subtitle
textil textiles
tidning newspaper
tidningskiosk newsstand
tidsschema schedule [timetable BE]
till to
tills until
tillåta v allow
timme hour
toalett bathroom [toilet BE]
toalettpapper toilet paper
tobaksaffär tobacconist
tofflor slippers
tolk interpreter
top peak (moutain)
torg square (town feature)
trappa stair
trasig broken (damaged)
trevlig pleasant
trist boring
tryck push
trådlös internet wireless internet

trä wood
träffa v meet
träfigur wood carvings
träkniv wooden knife
träningsmassage sports massage
träningsskor sneakers
träsked wooden spoon
träskor wooden clogs
tröja sweater
tugga v chew
tull customs
tulldeklaration customs declaration form
tunnelbana subway [underground BE]
tunnelbanestation subway station [underground station BE]
tur tour
turist tourist
turist klass economy class
turistattraktion tourist attraction
turistbyrå tourist office
turistinformation tourist information
tvål soap
tvätt laundry
tvättmaskin washing machine
tvättmedel laundry detergent
tvättmöjligheter laundry facilities
tyg fabric
tyvärr unfortunately

tåg train
täcke n blanket
tältsäng camping bed
tändare lighter
tändsticka match (fire)
tänka v think

U

ull wool
underhållning entertainment
underkläder underwear (general)
undersöka v examine (medical)
undertäckna v sign
upprepa v repeat
upptagen busy
ursäkta v excuse me (to get attention, pardon me)
ursäkta mig excuse me (to get past)
ute outside
utgång exit way out
utländsk valuta foreign currency
utomhus outdoor
utomhusbassäng outdoor pool
utrikes international (travel)
utrustning equipment
utsiktspunkt view point
utslag n rash
uttag withdrawal (bank)

V

vacker beautiful

vaginal infektion vaginal infection
vakna v wake up
valuta currency
vandra v hike
vandrarhem youth hostel
vandring hiking
vanlig regular gas
var where
var god stör ej do not disturb
vara v be
varje each
varm hot
varsågod (invitation) please
varuhus department store
vaskrensare plunger
vattenfall waterfall
WC (sign) restroom [toilet BE]
veckotidning magazine
vegetarian vegetarian
vem who
vid at
vilja v want
vilken which
vilse lost
visa v show
vitrin display case
vitt white
vykort postcard
våldtäkt n rape
våning floor (level, etage in building)
våtservetter för barn baby wipes

väderleksrapport weather forecast
väg road
vägkarta road map
välkommen welcome
välling baby formula
vän friend
vänster left (direction)
vänta wait
värde n value
värdesak n valuable
värme heat
väska bag
väster west
växel n change (money)
växelkontor currency exchange office
växelkursen exchange rate
växla change money

Y

yr dizzy
ytterliggare further (more)

Å

å stream
åka v travel, drive (motor vehicle)
åksjuka motion sickness [travel sickness BE]
ålder age
återlämna v return (give back)
äkta authentic